Martin Keenan takes us on his absorbing life journey with total honesty and transparency. Facing rejection as a child and uncertainty in his teenage years Martin's story will help many searching for security, purpose and direction in their lives. Written in an uncomplicated free flowing style, this clear and thoughtful book weaves together fibres of raw pain within the context 1960s, 70s, and 80s culture and offsets them with random moments of humour and wit.

This narrative is written with the core message being that of Christian redemption. but within a context that offers hope and meaningfulness to any reader.

Colin Murray

Christian faith writer and author of 'Papering Over The Cracks'

To Margaret

(Romans 8v28)

Martin

I'm humbled to endorse Martin Keenan's book, "Accepted...at last." Only in silence could Martin find a place to feel his pain and question his own existence. A deep-seated fear of rejection kept him silent to the world. With a mind close to genius, he agonized over his Raison d'etre, his reason for being and found nothing.

Being a polar opposite from Martin, I struggled and failed to break through that wall. Love was my only attack. Clearly blinded, Martin had been seeking for something that had been there from the beginning of time.

In a candid journey with no holds barred, Martin's feelings explode across the pages of what it felt like to be rejected from his biological family, adopted without knowing love, a chronic loner, and a highly intelligent youth with an inability to communicate. He was a man who kept his pain of rejection and loneliness buried so deep that no one could break through except the Great I AM, the same who gave a tongue to stuttering Moses and prophetic words for the young Jeremiah to speak. Hidden deep in Martin's brilliance was a precious diamond waiting to be unearthed. Only God, the Great Transformer, could turn this mute teen into a witty theologian full of passion for Christ and accepted among the beloved. Romans 15:7

Skip Ball
Author of Stronghold

Accepted... at Last

Martin Keenan

Matador
9 Priory Business Park
Kibworth Beauchamp
Leicestershire LE8 0RX, UK
Tel: (+44) 116 279 2299
Fax: (+44) 116 279 2277
Email: books@troubador.co.uk
Web: www.troubador.co.uk/matador

ISBN 978 1780885 506

British Library Cataloguing in Publication Data.
A catalogue record for this book is available from the British Library.

Typeset in Book Antiqua by Troubador Publishing Ltd
Printed and bound in the UK by TJ International, Padstow, Cornwall

Matador is an imprint of Troubador Publishing Ltd

For Tamar

Chapter one

In the beginning...

This is the story of my life. It's not a typical testimony story: I was a sinner, God saved me and life has been wonderful ever since. It's the story of my life. I don't tell everything that happened to me. Some things are left out, but I tell the stories that show how I became who I am today. It is told from my point of view (naturally). If anyone else wrote it they would tell it differently. But this is me telling you who I am. I hope it helps!

My life began in a less than glorious way. I was the product of an adulterous liaison between a 20 year old country girl from Cumbria and a married man from who knows where. The conception took place in the seaside resort of Morecambe. The result was that I was born in "*Saint Monica's Home for Unmarried Mothers*" in Kendal, Cumbria and then adopted through official channels by a couple in Runcorn, Cheshire.

I discovered that my mother herself was the product of an adulterous liaison between an unmarried country man from Cumbria and a married woman from the same village. Granddad was a postman in the village and grandma was married with 3 children. Her husband left – I don't know the details, but I do know that there must have been a divorce eventually because by the time grandma and granddad got married the wedding certificate recorded her status as: *'Previous marriage dissolved'*. In the meantime they lived together in their tiny village in Cumbria. Apparently they never knew about my existence. I was born in January 1962, just 2 months after my mother's 21st birthday and granddad and grandma were married at the end of February 1962.

And on the 26th March 1962 I was handed over to a new family, which included a two year old boy who had also been adopted. For most of my life I believed that my mother had given me a teddy bear (a panda to be precise) and a children's Book of Prayers and a children's Christian song book. When I eventually reunited with her 40 years later she claimed no knowledge of these 'gifts', so I now have no idea where they came from, but it was disappointing to think that all my life these had been my links with her and I had been lied to. I still have them, as my only links with my previous life.

If you read anything about adoption and the trauma involved then you will know how traumatic that day (26th March 1962) was for me. The best book I have read on the subject is "*Primal Wound*" by Nancy Verrier. Those who say that adoption does not affect children are usually those who have not been adopted – and I have met many people who have told me that I should ignore the fact that I was adopted and be grateful that I had a family. Comparisons with orphans and abused children would be paraded in front of me to demonstrate how I had 'no right' to be affected by my mother abandoning me and anyway, it was a long time ago and I probably wasn't aware of it. The truth is, I was there when it happened. I don't remember it, but I grew up with a fear of rejection that affected my everyday life every day of my life. I always had the feeling of not belonging. In my darker moments of childhood I felt like I had been kidnapped and was lost, which, apparently is normal in adopted children. There is an incident reported in Nancy Verrier's book that really touched me, so I'll quote it here:

"One woman told me that she had intended to write a long letter to her birthmother about whom she had no conscious memory but for whom she had been thinking about searching. She wanted to explain how she felt about being adopted. She decided to write with her left hand, because she had heard that this would access her right brain and put her more in touch with her feelings. Taking pen in hand, she wrote: "Dear Mommy, Come and get me." After that, she told me, there seemed to be nothing more to say."

Throughout my childhood I felt homesick and that is a feeling that has never really left. Nowadays I can theologise and say I am homesick for Eden, along with the rest of the human race, but at the time when I was in Primary School it was a feeling that occasionally

3

overwhelmed me. And maybe the theological explanation is true, but the emotional explanation is equally valid.

Nancy Verrier quotes studies that argue that bonding doesn't begin at birth; it begins *in utero* during those first 9 months of life. To quote: *'When this natural evolution is interrupted by a postnatal separation from the biological mother, the resultant experience of abandonment and loss is indelibly printed upon the unconscious minds of these children…'*

So how does it feel to be handed over to strangers? Suddenly to be surrounded by strangers with no sign of mother! No wonder I felt like I had been kidnapped. Apparently there is a common fantasy among adoptees that they will one day be rescued. It was a relief to read about that because it was a fantasy with which I grew up and it does lead to fears of insanity.

I don't remember being told that I was adopted, but I imagine it was before I started school at the age of 5. Before that I was apparently fairly talkative. I used to escape from the garden and go for walks, being returned by complete strangers, having directed them back to my house (it was a very different world!) After I started school I didn't speak for years. It was assumed by some that I hadn't learned how to speak. Fortunately for me there were no School Psychologists or SENCOs in those days otherwise my life may have been more traumatic than it was.

The story I was told was that my mother was very

young and she lived with her parents. She worked as a secretary and because of me she couldn't work, so she gave me away because her parents couldn't afford to keep me. None of this was true as I have already revealed, and as will be revealed later.

I can only write this from my own memories and as I don't have access to anyone else's memories, or the ability to assess anyone else's motives I cannot comment on why things happened, except when they were explained to me. I was told about my adoption because my adopted mum's uncle had been adopted and he only discovered the fact when he went for a job interview. He never spoke to his family again. And so it was better for me to hear the news at home rather than in the playground. And in case you are wondering – yes it was talked about in the playground. We didn't have geeks and nerds, we had adopted kids. I remember being told that I had no real family; I remember being mocked for being adopted instead of born. At least it was an original form of bullying!

As for why I was adopted: this is a question that isn't asked in polite society. And so I never questioned it, until I was in university doing my Sociology degree when one of the lecturers said that the question, "Why do people have children?" was never asked. The usual question was to ask a couple without children why they didn't conform. But why have children? Well, I had always thought in my case that it was just the thing to do and as most of my parents' siblings had children, maybe they didn't want to be left out. Then a few years ago, in an angry moment, my dad said that the only reason he had adopted us was so that he would have children or grandchildren to look after him in his old age. This explains his annoyance when I moved out of my home town.

One major problem I had as a child was with that Social Services line about: '*Tell them that they are special because they were chosen*". I had a problem with that because if I was so special why did my mother reject me before I was born? This also is common I have discovered. We know we couldn't be special; we know there is something inherently wrong with us, otherwise our mothers would not abandon us to strangers. But it seemed to satisfy everyone else so I didn't object. In fact, I didn't object to anything. I developed the psychological defence mechanism known as 'Withdrawal'. I withdrew into my own fantasy world which felt much safer. Apparently there had been some of this withdrawal in my pre-school days as well. When I was ill I never said what was wrong with me; I just groaned and cried. But the fantasy world grew.

The real world had a lot more people in it and they mostly seemed hostile, but that was more about me than them. In Infant School I was in a class of 45 children. I have vague memories: I wouldn't drink the daily bottle of milk. When I was asked why not I wouldn't say. The teacher called my brother in to try to persuade me as I

6

liked milk, but I wouldn't tell him why I wouldn't drink it either. My reasons were that I wouldn't drink out of a bottle and I only like cold milk, but I couldn't tell them for fear of ridicule. I went through all my school life without drinking school milk.

Also I remember when we did Art and I was one of several in the class who always forgot to put my name on my drawings or paintings, so the teacher used to hold up our pictures and ask who they belonged to. I never claimed mine. I imagine it was obvious to the teacher whose they were, but I was always ashamed to admit to my own handiwork, because I didn't want to be laughed at, or criticised. It was years before I discovered how artistic I was.

Most memories are vague from my younger days – I remember always trying to make sure I had money if we went on a family shopping trip by train to places like Liverpool or Manchester. There was always the fear of being abandoned again and so I wanted the money to get back home … to the people who I thought were trying to abandon me. I know! Logic hadn't developed at this stage.

I am not going to write about what happened in my private fantasy world, because it remains private. And it doesn't explain anything. But it helped me get through my childhood, so my thanks to all my imaginary friends wherever you may be.

But there was one major fear that developed when I

was 9 years old. This was 1971 and in our class at school the teacher taught us about the Bible and taught us to recite the Lord's Prayer. This was the start of my existential fear. I discovered there was a God I should pray to and there were certain words I had to pray to this God. I remember going home from the lesson on the Bible and asking my mum if she had a Bible. She did and so I started reading the King James Version, beginning in Genesis. I read a chapter a day and then reached Deuteronomy 23. Verse 2 traumatised me. Here it is: '*A bastard shall not enter into the congregation of the LORD; even to his tenth generation shall he not enter into the congregation of the LORD.*'

And my first attempt at Bible interpretation was not as good as my present efforts. I took it to mean that because of the circumstances of my conception I wouldn't get to heaven. This is when I developed a fear of death, as well as the belief that God rejected me. I didn't have a hope. Imagine how I felt when I heard that idea that your schooldays are the happiest days of your life. At this stage I was too scared of what might happen next to be suicidal, although I went through long periods of wishing I had never been born. Life was filled with fear and there was nowhere to turn for help. There were nights when I would be terrified of falling asleep in case I woke up in hell. I would try and keep myself awake as long as I could. The thought that I could die while I was awake didn't occur to me!

My next clear memory was sitting my 11+ exam. By this stage I was so unaware of what was happening in the real world that the first I knew about the exam was when I went into my classroom and there was a sign on the door that said: *'Exam in Progress'*. I may have been unaware, but I wasn't stupid and I passed. That was a relief to me because at the age of 9 I had grown my hair long and the one major difference I knew between the Grammar School and Balfour Road Secondary School was that you could keep your hair long at the Grammar School. There was also the fact that Balfour Road Secondary School had its fair share of unsavoury characters and the chances of getting beaten up were quite high. I have two memories of this kind of trouble. Once I was at Runcorn hills with my brother when a couple of older boys who had just been released from Borstal attacked us. They wanted to make my brother cry, but he was a bit stubborn and took all that they gave him. Me, well, I was different then. They picked me up and threw me into a gorse bush. I was rescued by a girl who was with them. I've always preferred girls and I guess it started there! Yes, I cried! The next time was when a gang of Scousers attacked me and some people I was with – same place, but this time they threw stones at us. I've sympathised with Stephen the first Christian martyr ever since – stoning hurts!

When I was 11 I went on my first holiday away from the family. This was a school trip to Belgium and Holland for a long weekend in May. I can remember the fear I felt as I was going to be away just for a few days. Maybe this is normal, but if you read the research it is something that affects adopted children a lot worse because of the fear of separation. It really was a mixed up childhood. I didn't like going away on family holidays because those annual 2 week holidays were the only time we spent together and it took me away from everything that had become familiar. Apart from that, any time the holiday went wrong I was always blamed for it. We used to go to cafes and my dad would read the menu in the window, announce that there was nothing on the menu I would eat and then have a go at me for making my mum cook when she was supposed to be having a rest. It was a delight when I was older to actually get to read a menu and try all this food I hadn't been allowed to try before!

Anyway, Grammar School! I remember getting the results of my 11+ and riding my bike (a Chopper – naturally) up to some friends' houses (I use the term 'friend' lightly). They had all passed and they had been promised presents from their parents. I went home and my news was given a different reception. Two years earlier my brother had failed his 11+exam, so I was told that if I ever used my success against him I would be taken out of the school. As for a present, I was told that I was getting a briefcase (school regulation briefcase – mandatory). I don't recall being congratulated by anyone. I would have been accepted more if I had failed.

But that was life and I was used to it – just another brick in the wall! And so I found myself in a big school, having to travel by school bus with a lot of strangers. This being put with strangers didn't seem to stop. I used to walk to the bus stop and stand by myself while everyone else was in their huddles. I would get on the bus and sit by myself (usually next to someone, but by myself) and then walk up to the boys' part of the school and drift into my safe world. I was only there a couple of days before I was set upon by a very old and very aggressive teacher because we had just come out of PE and I'd had to fasten my tie, which I had never done by myself before. My top button was undone and my tie was not straight. I discovered that this was the unforgivable sin in a Grammar School. My inability to sort it out was ridiculed and my non-existent self-esteem popped up to tell me it was never coming back.

And to add insult to insult I lost my class. The room we were supposed to be in was empty and they had been relocated to somewhere else. The nightmare continued!

On the social side I was in the park around this time with some other acquaintances when an older boy asked me which school I attended. When I told him he asked if I wanted a fight. When I declined he called me a coward (or some colloquial equivalent). It was a really serious offence to pass the 11+ exam!

And I was given a name at school: 'Mr. Speak'. For the first two years I really didn't have much to say. I had no friends and the teachers were bullies, complete with '*dark sarcasm in the classroom*' and because of my being quiet I was an easy target for bullying teachers to pick on. It used to puzzle me why being quiet was so wrong. The loud and aggressives were challenged, but the quiet ones were bullied. There was one occasion where my parents actually came to the rescue. Of all lessons in which to get the worst bullying it was my RE teacher who excelled. And it obviously showed at home, because my parents asked me what was wrong with me. When I told them about my bullying teacher they went straight to the school. My dad could be very determined back then and while I don't know what they said I know that the teacher was scared. He couldn't be nicer to me after that. That was my first break in the nightmare that was my schooldays.

But my 13th birthday was coming up. I was about to become a teenager. I discovered sex when I was 12 – well, hard-core porn to be precise. A boy who lived down the road from us discovered that under his parents' mattress there were some amazing glossy magazines of things we couldn't have even imagined. That can have quite a damaging effect on someone at any age, but at the age of 12…

Anyway, I hadn't been 13 very long before I met the police. I was going to one of our many parks and I picked up a sign that had blown down and the next thing I hear is a police siren and there's the police car and the police hassling me for touching the sign. I felt like there was a sign on my head that said, *Teenager; treat with malice*. My first run-in with the law!

But then I was to spend that summer (1975) in hospital. My little toes are bent inward and the nails were cutting my other toes so it was decided I should go to hospital to have my toes broken and straightened. I was in for 4 hours before they decided it wasn't worth doing and I was sent home. I'm being deliberately vague here; I don't know who 'they' were, but they were making a lot of decisions about me. 'They' seemed to always be making decisions about me. One of my desires was to grow up quickly so that 'they' would no longer be able to dictate to me who I should be and where I should be it. It was a long time before that happened.

If I had stayed in hospital I wouldn't have had my psychological conversion that summer and I wouldn't have transformed into the person I became.

As it was I found myself in a party with my brother and a friend of his from down the road. The party was in one of the 'no-go' areas. It was a rough town! I don't know what I was doing there. My brother's girlfriend (who became his first wife) lived in that area and this party was at his friend's girlfriend's house. There was an incident at the party when a local gang wanted us to send someone out to them – a fugitive from their justice. My brother told them to go away (again, colloquial equivalent is assumed).

And then we had to go home. Through Indian country! We hadn't got far before this gang caught up with us and one of them produced a knife. They were not happy with my brother. He got into an argument with them and while that was happening, his very brave friend was edging to the corner of the road. He whispered to me to join him. To my shame (which lasted for several years after) I joined him and at the corner we ran, being chased by a couple of members of this gang. My brother, meanwhile, fought off the rest of them. He was pretty tough. He caught up with us and didn't seem to mind that we had left him.

I did! I couldn't forgive myself for my cowardice. This was like the final straw in the bullying that I had had to put up with all my life. In my parents' bedroom there was a dressing table with a big mirror. I used to sit and talk to that mirror (when no one was in). It was the only chance I ever had to unload, because the mirror was a good listener. Well, shortly after this incident this mirror and I had a good long talk and I made some decisions: never again was I going to be bullied; never again was I going to walk away from a fight or a threat; no one was ever going to push me around – ever. And it wasn't just empty words. I changed radically and it was noticed. I also decided that I would buy a toothbrush and start cleaning my teeth as this was something I hadn't done much of before. Did I mention that my dentist was a bully as well? He used to shout at me when I went for

14

check-ups. He would offer me a sweet and I would tell him I didn't like sweets, so he would shout at me and tell me that all children like sweets and make me take it. The only other bully I can remember was the swimming teacher in the local swimming pool. She threw me in at the deep end more than once. People like that would be fired from their jobs nowadays, but back then bullying was allowed. And the more quiet and withdrawn the child, the easier the target.

This leads to one redeeming and one condemning story. My mum decided she would teach me to swim so that I wouldn't have such a difficult time at school swimming lessons. The problem with this idea was that she had a perforated ear drum and wasn't allowed to get her ear wet. Well, she did and so her hearing was affected for the rest of her life.

I did eventually learn to swim at evening swimming classes and it was decided that I should swim "the length" (25 yards). We had no telephone at this point and so the neighbour who had taken me swimming ran out to a phone box to phone another neighbour to tell my mum and dad to come and watch. My mum drove down and was there to cheer me on before I finished. My dad said he would only take an interest in my swimming if I learnt to dive. I haven't got around to mentioning that my secondary personality adaptation is 'Passive-Aggression' – I never learnt to dive; deliberately.

Anyway, I started hanging around with my brother's

15

brave friend shortly after this fight incident in 1975. His girlfriend had dumped him and so he had no one else. Both his parents worked so we spent the rest of that summer holiday in his house and he introduced me to groups like Deep Purple and Black Sabbath. This was the start of my interest in Rock and other music and the start of my attending Rock Concerts in Liverpool Empire. In the evenings we used to hang around the streets writing our names on bus stops and walls with marker pens. I had become a vandal! I used to peel off the new signs that the council were putting up everywhere: 'Keep Britain Tidy'. I had a collection of them. But then the gang mentioned earlier moved into our territory and I started to have some fun at everyone else's expense. This new friend of mine liked to act tough with me, but I knew he was a coward. He was a lot bigger than me and he would occasionally use his strength against me, but then this gang would appear and he would want to sink into the shadows. I, on the other hand, developed a fixed stare that has been a lifetime affliction. I used to stare at them and then say in a voice louder than I was supposed to have: 'What are they looking at? They're looking at us'. My cowardly friend used to cringe with fear. I discovered later that this gang respected my brother, for having beaten them; they knew my friend was a coward; but they were afraid of me because they couldn't understand why I wasn't scared of them. Things were looking up. A year or so later I heard from one of the tougher kids in my class that no one threatened me because they found it humiliating. They thought they could beat me in a fight but if they ever threatened me I used to laugh at them. And that was humiliating.

I tried to get some of my school friends to stand up for themselves, but that usually left me standing alone in the face of danger.

I never had to have a fight, I just stared at people and that was enough. But then when I was 15 I went outside my comfort zone and found myself in dangerous territory. We started hanging out in Shopping City, which was Britain's first indoor shopping arcade and a place where all kinds of bad people hung out. I encountered an older teenager who threatened to kill me as he was going to jail for several years – he just didn't like me, but that wasn't new to find someone who didn't like me for being me. I didn't think it deserved the death penalty though. My new friends advised me to stay away until he was inside, but I had made myself a promise. There was the one fight I had. My town was a dangerous place and there were girl gangs and boy gangs. If you had the choice you would be better facing up to a boy gang. The girls were vicious. Anyway, my fight made my friends wary of me. I had only ever fought my brother during childhood. My one and only fight as a teenager was enough to make people keep their distance. I lost all consciousness in the fight and went wild. Then there was the thug and his friends who stole my scarf and wanted me to try and take it back. There were three of them and one of me. As I said, I wasn't completely stupid, so I put up with his name calling and let him keep the scarf.

I got my first girlfriend at this time. She was Scouse, she was completely immoral; her name was Sue, she was 12 and she had already had an abortion, and the relationship lasted a whole week. I had had my first kiss a few weeks earlier at a drunken party – it was a Cider flavoured kiss.

But my Shopping City days soon came to an end. My friend left school and got a job and new friends. I decided I'd had enough of going out. I hadn't redeemed myself yet, but I was taking a break from redemption and was losing myself in music. I had always been fairly artistic (except at Primary School, as mentioned earlier) and I discovered hippies around this time, and a couple of hippy shops. I started embroidering pictures from record covers onto my jeans and became very much an out-of-date flower-power person. Much to the absolute annoyance of my parents. They thought I should have cut my hair by now and should be spending time with friends. My dad's usual low opinion of me was that I thought I was too good for everyone and that was why I didn't go out. So in the evenings they made me go out and walk the streets. It wasn't too long before he was complaining that I '*treat(ed) the house like a hotel*'. I was never sure what the game was, but I knew I could never win.

But it was difficult treating it like a home as I was beginning to feel more and more of an outsider. This was compounded at the age of 15 when my dad told me I was no member of his family. That was not the best thing I had been told. The reason he said it was because I was different. I didn't act like a natural member of the family. They liked things I didn't; I liked things they didn't. I just didn't fit and so I had to be told. I was also told that I needed to start thinking about applying for jobs when I left school at 16 because they were not going to be around to support me forever (34 years later and they are still around!) There was no mention of me staying on to do A-Levels and go to university. It was bad enough that I had passed the 11+ without getting A-Levels and a degree! My problem was that there was nothing that I wanted to do for the rest of my life. I was interested in the hippies who lived in the Welsh mountains and then there were the people who lived in canal boats in the town. I liked the idea of being a photographer; I also wanted to go to Art College in Chester. All of these suggestions were dismissed. The Careers Advice at school was either get a job in a bank or get an apprenticeship. This was the Industrial North-West of England where ICI dominated, so it was expected. Also, my dad worked for ICI in a semi-skilled job – Foreman Rigger; my brother had failed to get into ICI and now was an apprentice electrician working for an Electrical Contractor. I had *brains* so I should be able to get into

ICI with no trouble at all. What these people without *'brains'* didn't realise was that I don't have a technical cell in my brain. But somehow I got into ICI as an apprentice Instrument Artificer.

And so I had a long summer between leaving school and starting to work at a job that we were advised would have to last us until we were 65 years old when we could retire.

During that summer my quest for redemption began again. I started hanging around with some friends from school. Actually, in the daytime I hung around with one of them (the others had all fallen out with him) and in the evening I hung around with the rest. My daytime friend was a worse hippy-type than I was. This was the summer of joss-sticks, patchouli oil and the odd whiff of pot.

I soon gave up hanging around with these new friends – soon after they were all reconciled. They all started going to pubs and although I wasn't opposed to alcohol, having been drunk on several occasions, I didn't like the idea that this was the rest of my life: work all day; pub all evening. So once again I was by myself. And I was walking the streets again. My home town was a kind of microcosm of everything that came out of the '60s and '70s – we had hippy types; Mods with their scooters; rockers with their motorbikes; skinheads with no fashion sense at all. The town was generally divided between those who like Rock music and those who like Northern Soul, so the Wigan Pier brigade were another feature.

I used to go for walks in my embroidered jeans, kaftans, or khurtas and Afghan coat, looking for trouble, but not initiating it. No matter where I went I never found trouble. Even if I saw a gang of skinheads walking towards me and I crossed over to walk through them they just ignored me. I guess God was looking out for me even when I wasn't aware of him.

There was the time a biker friend of mine was attacked by a gang of Mods; I spent a week hanging out at the place where he was attacked, but they never came back.

My new job was awful. I hated being an apprentice. I had no idea what I was doing most of the time and I was useless at everything I was supposed to do. One of the projects we had to do resulted in me getting a fail and the comment: *'Worst ever!'* But I developed a new set of friends. We started going to the cinema in Widnes occasionally. But I was still walking the streets alone in the meantime.

I had a lot of hang-ups at this time. If adolescence hadn't been invented by Bill Haley I would have had to invent it for myself. There had to have been some explanation for my teenage angst/anomie/alienation and adolescence covered it all. I read a very old Psychology encyclopaedia when I was 17 and I was convinced at the end of it that I needed to see a psychiatrist. I heard later – much later – that this is a normal reaction when first reading psychology. If I had read about the traumatic effects of adoption at the time I probably would have tried to get myself committed!

It was getting difficult being alone and I was starting to experience the Twilight Zone all by myself. My private world was very strange and even when I was with other people, where I was able to be the comedian with the quick one-liners and the ability to spot an innuendo in any conversation, I still went home and cried myself to sleep at nights.

But things were about to change – again!

Chapter two

In the beginning was the word...

One Sunday evening, during my solitary walks I found myself in an area I didn't know too well and I came across someone I had vaguely known at school, so I started talking to him. He was sitting on the steps of a building and he said that he was waiting for the youth club to open. I had tried a youth club once before in a church hall – Welsh Presbyterian as it turned out. It was a grotty place with grotty equipment, but it was somewhere to go. The man who ran it did what he called a '*God-slot*' at the end of each night. I remember telling my mum about that when I got home, and then trying to persuade her that I had actually found it interesting. I was reading all kinds of stuff at this time: pyramids, sacred stones, pop psychology. The Christian terminology would be that I was '*searching*'. We got in trouble in that youth club because we went into the church and were messing around with the pews and organ and other things. And the minister went to everyone's house to tell our parents! Like I said, it was a different world.

Anyway, I decided to try this youth club because there was a girl who went to it who I had liked when I was at school. She wasn't there that night, but I hung around and the leader of the group asked me if I wanted to play table tennis. I have no memory of this, but she told everyone for years afterwards that I took my shoes off to play. My answer was always that I had never played table tennis before, but I assumed it wasn't right to be on the table in shoes – no idea what my real reason was. She also said I gave monosyllabic answers to her questions, which she found difficult. Somehow I managed to fit in a little in this group. It was 1979 and a few of these kids, and the leader (who was in her late 20s) had become Christians. It turned out that the building I was in was a church – Methodist. The system was that every other week the group met in the minister's house. That was a weird place. I didn't know anything about any church, so the whole idea of circuits was foreign to me, but I eventually got to meet what I guess was the rest of that circuit's ministers – they all smoked pipes! For years afterwards that was all I knew about the Methodist Church – the ministers smoke pipes.

Anyway, on that first evening the radio was on (I never listened to the radio) and a new story was being played: '*The Hitchhiker's Guide to the Galaxy*'. I loved it. I didn't get to hear much of it, but as soon as the books were published I would buy them and read them. One of my earliest influences as a Christian was the atheist author of '*Hitchhikers*' – Douglas Adams!

There was a topic to discuss at these meetings and that night we were to answer the question: *'Where do you see yourself 10 years from now?'* That is a question no one could answer. I was 17 years old. I'd never been to a church service. I knew all the Bible stories and I had a Grade C O-Level in Religious Education (The life of Jesus in the Synoptic Gospels). I had been to one evangelistic meeting a year before, where we watched the film, *The Cross and the Switchblade*. I found it really boring and months later when the film, *The Warriors* was on at the cinema I found that a lot more entertaining. I knew nothing about Christianity at all. I was terrified of speaking in public and wouldn't even answer the question in a small group. But ten years after that meeting, in September 1989 I was back at Theological College finishing my degree in Theology, preaching at a college service.

My job was changing at this point as well. The first year of the apprenticeship was spent at the training centre in Widnes. That involved a bus trip to work each day with all these old, yellowed, men coughing up their insides as they smoked themselves to death. I decided that this wasn't to be my future, but I had no way out. There was also the system of block release at technical college, so it was six weeks at the training centre and then six weeks at college. But then after the first year we went into the real factories. And then I went back to not speaking. I hated it and that was my usual response to situations I hated: withdrawal. I had been the group comedian for the first year, but that ended. I saved it for what became the day-release days at college for the next three years.

My job became a question of following a tradesman around while he did his job. It wasn't long before I was in trouble for not showing any interest in anything that was happening. No one asked me if I was interested; they just assumed. I was being quiet and they didn't like that. My personality wasn't accepted, again. I was told at the official (annual) meetings that I should be asking questions. So I started asking how things worked and my tradesmen could never answer those questions, so I gave up asking, and then got into more trouble. There was a tradition among tradesmen that apprentices were easy prey for perverted pleasures in an attempt to humiliate us. There was a blue dye that was used that was indelible. The goal was to strip the apprentice and paint his genitals. When I heard about that I started carrying around my big adjustable spanner in one of the long pockets in my overalls and my Stillson wrench in the other pocket. I was armed and dangerous and no one was going to paint me. And fortunately, for them and me, no one tried. But I never left home without them!

As I said, I was encountering Christians now and they were a varied group of people. There was one at work and he was the oddest oddball of them all. There was nothing about them that made me think: 'I want what they've got'. All I thought was: '*Keep me away from those weirdos*'. And every night I prayed the Lord's Prayer at top speed just in case I died in my sleep. This was my new superstition. I thought God would overlook the circumstances of my conception if I said these magical words just before I died.

And then it was Christmas Eve 1979. I was invited by the youth club leader to a pub about two miles from home. It was lunch time. I hadn't eaten and I got completely plastered. I had to walk home alone. I don't know how I managed it, but there wasn't as much traffic back then, so I managed to cross all the roads safely. I got home and crashed on my bed, waking occasionally through the rest of the evening and all night to throw up in the toilet.

And did I get any trouble for this obvious demonstration of under-age drinking? Not at all. For once I had done something right. The only comment was that I would learn to pace myself in the future. I don't remember that Christmas Day at all, but, shortly after, the youth club leader lent me a copy of the book, '*The Cross and the Switchblade*'. I had forgotten about the film and I found the book very absorbing. But then I still prefer the book version to the film version of any story. When Nicky Cruz became a Christian in the book I thought: '*I want that*'. But I didn't know what to do about it. As far as I was aware at that point, I didn't know any Christians to help me, and pipe-smoking ministers were like bullying school teachers from what I could see, so I wouldn't have dreamt of going to them for help. What do church ministers know about salvation?

So I prayed. I had never prayed in my life until now. Well, I always had my fear prayers. I was always worried about being abandoned again, so when the fear got bad I used to pray that my family would all die in a car crash together, or in a gas explosion, just so I wouldn't be left alone. Does that count as praying?

Anyway I had no idea what to say to this God who didn't want me down to the 10th generation, but I reasoned that if Nicky Cruz could get saved (whatever that entailed) then so could I. So I prayed my deeply theological sinner's prayer: *'God, make me a Christian'*. And He did.

I couldn't have told anyone what had happened to me if I had been questioned, but something changed within me. The biggest thing was the relief. There is a verse that fits what happened, in the King James Version – Ephesians 1: 6 'accepted in the beloved'. I felt accepted at last. It took years to fully understand that, but the immediate relief was enough. I was accepted, not rejected. It was also a while before I found that verse in Isaiah where God expresses his surprise that a mother could abandon her child, and then He says that even if that should happen He would never abandon me – I took it personally and it helped (Isaiah 49: 15 *'Can a woman forget her nursing child, or show no compassion for the child*

of her womb? Even these may forget, yet I will not forget you.'
(NRSV)).

One of the big changes that I noticed was when I was out walking one night and there was a gang walking towards me – I stepped off the pavement onto the road instead of walking through them. I did it without thinking and I was amazed. My death wish was over.

As soon as I could I went to Chester and bought a Bible in W.H. Smiths – a Good News Bible. I didn't know there were different versions of the Bible and I had no idea about Christian bookshops. But I read that Bible at every opportunity. I would take it to the bath and read a minor prophet – I had no idea how to read it and no one to guide me. The baths got longer when I read books like Hosea; I was a wrinkled prune sitting in cold water when I read Daniel. I was aware that I had no idea what most of it was about, but I couldn't get enough of it.

And somehow I got my hands on some Christian autobiographies and biographies. I began reading about the Christian life; how Christians related to each other and what the Church was and what it was all about. And I would go to the youth club and wonder why these new Christians, most of whom had grown up going to church, were nothing like the Christians I was reading about in the books. They had started a Bible study that they ran themselves and so I went one night. The comment I heard when the door was opened to me was, *'What's he doing here?'* I wasn't welcome! Church was for church people, not people like me. But I knew God had accepted me so I persisted. God wanted me, but the Church didn't. So a bit of acceptance and a bit of the usual rejection.

Anyway, I persisted in going to this Bible Study – not the best thing to do. I started attending the church as well. I don't remember anything much about it. The minister waffled about his holidays on the Isle of Dogs and said we had to be nice. I've been trying to formulate a "Doctrine of Niceness" for a few years now. Maybe I should look that minister up for some advice. Anyway there was one service that was communion. We had to go up to the front of the church. I had bells sewn to the bottom of my embroidered jeans so I jingled up to the front and I was told it was an amusing sight – I looked like an angel in my white embroidered khurta (if you don't know what that is yet look it up). Next to me was Andy, who I'd met on the steps. He was wearing his AC/DC concert t-shirt. The tour had been promoting their new album: 'Highway to Hell', but at least we weren't thrown out!

The youth Bible Study was led by a different person each week. It began with singing from a paperback book. I didn't know any of the songs and I didn't sing. Jane, one of the girls from a good Christian family, really didn't like me being there. One week she was passing out the song books and she threw mine at me saying, '*I don't know why I'm giving you this, you don't sing anyway.*' I was a Christian at this point. It really was a good job, because they wouldn't have liked me if they'd made me angry. But I prayed instead (thanking God for paperback songbooks!). I remember one week asking God to let me get on with Jane – either that or arrange it that she wouldn't be there. As the Bible says, '*If it is possible, as far as it depends on you, be at peace with everyone*'. She wasn't there! Result! The next week I forgot to pray, and there she was. So I remembered the following week and she wasn't there again. This was getting really good. But then after a few months they decided I should lead the Bible Study. I have to say that at this point I had a reputation for being scared of no one, but I was terrified of speaking in public. I had been a comedian and comedy I could do, but not formally. Anyway, it was a church group, so it was bound to be friendly. I had a lot to learn and I learnt most of it in that group.

I didn't know how to study the Bible. I had discovered Christian bookshops by this time and I had bought a book on Ezekiel, called, '*All things weird and wonderful*'. The title appealed to me. I don't remember what I prepared, but a day before the Bible Study I had a feeling that I should look up something different. I've been inspired a lot over the last couple of decades, but it was a new experience, and so I looked up **Romans 8: 1** and I was fascinated. So I went to the Bible Study with questions, not answers. This has become my normal means of communication: ask me a question and I'll ask you one back. So I asked if, '*There is now no condemnation* *for those who are in Christ Jesus'* means that Christians go to heaven. Seriously! I have 3 degrees in Theology now and I have read through the Bible more times than I can remember. I know all the doctrines of the Christian faith (Niceness is coming along... nicely!), but back then I knew nothing! I knew that God had accepted me, but hell was still looming as far as I was aware. But this looked like the New Testament might overrule the Old Testament. It does, in case you were wondering. Even eunuchs get in! I used to quote that verse about illegitimacy as Deuteronomy 23: 1 – look it up. It explains why people used to look at me in a strange way. But they get in as Acts tells us.

The response I got from my good Christian friends was, *'Don't be stupid, of course they do!'* On the way home (we got lifts from their parents, which fascinated me) one of the dads asked how it had gone and one of them said it was, *'Rubbish! The worst Bible Study I have ever been to'* as he laughed in my face. I decided then that I would never speak in a church again. I would just go and listen. But I knew I was definitely converted because I didn't even have the urge to hit this insensitive Christian. Augustine said it is one thing to turn the other cheek; it is another thing to love the person who hits you. I didn't love him, but I didn't feel the need to get back at him. A few years later I did get back at him accidentally, by making a flippant comment. I had gone to the youth club leader's house and he arrived. I said, *'If I'd known it was a party I wouldn't have come'*. He took it personally and was really upset. I heard that a long time later and I haven't seen him since.

Anyway, things were about to change for the better. People where I worked found out I had become a Christian and I became the subject of a bit of public ridicule and a bit of private questioning. I started to pray about this too. I asked God to get people to ask me why I was a Christian, and sure enough…

I should add another incident in here. I was an apprentice and in those days apprentices were treated like school kids. Parents had to sign the forms to say that they would ensure that their 'child' would fulfil all the requirements of the apprenticeship. There were annual meetings with the bosses as well. On one of these I was given a hard time over being a Christian. I was given a hard time each year, but this one was different and stands out in my memory. One of my bosses said to me, *'We hear you have an outside interest'*. It sounded ominous, so I sat looking at him saying nothing, so he said, *'We hear you are a Christian'*. Let me point out that at that time the Chairman of ICI was a Christian and there were at least three tradesmen I worked with who were Christians. There was also another apprentice who was a Christian. They knew about the other apprentice – he had grown up in a Christian family and he was extravert and sociable. I was new to being a Christian and still getting the hang of things. They compared me unfavourably to

33

him. Then they told me that I had to give up being a Christian! I could live like a Christian at home if I wanted to, but at work I had to give it up. If I continued to live like a Christian at work I would be in even more trouble. These bosses all knew my dad, so I imagine they talked to him about it, but I never heard anything about it. Not long after this one of these men died. I used to wonder what God said to him about that interview! But now I was being told that who I was was unacceptable because I was a Christian, not because I was me. This didn't have the usual effect that rejection had. It was Jesus in me that they objected to, so I saw this as Christian persecution.

Then one day someone I had vaguely known at school came to see me. He lived round the corner from me. Word of my conversion had spread – I wasn't that well-known, but somehow people heard. He told me about a new church that had started in the next town, led by an evangelist from California. He invited me along. George, as he was called (not his real name, just what he was called) was a biker, but he had bought a Reliant Robin. I had only just started taking driving lessons at this point. Never get into a car with a biker who drives a Reliant Robin! Three wheels! Dangerous! Anyway, we got to the church that met in Frodsham Community centre. The service lasted an hour and a half. I don't remember anything other than the fact that I wasn't bored. And the people were friendly. And this American was a Christian! He has written about this church in a book called 'Stronghold': available from Amazon. It's an amazing book and unless you were there you wouldn't believe the things that happened. I recommend the book!

So I was attending church twice on a Sunday in Frodsham, Bible Study on a Wednesday in Frodsham, Youth Club at the Methodist on a Thursday and Youth Fellowship in Frodsham on a Friday. During this first year as a Christian I went to quite a lot of evangelistic events in Warrington, Liverpool and various other places. I went on the MAYC London weekend with the Methodists. I discovered C.S. Lewis and Francis Schaeffer books as well as John Powell. I also discovered Cliff College. The idea of Bible Colleges was new to me as well. As I was hating my apprenticeship I thought maybe I could quit and go to Bible College. Cliff was the only one I had come across. But several people suggested that I finish my apprenticeship first. It was a 4 year apprenticeship and I was half way through it. Also, I read Paul's advice to slaves in the New Testament about staying in whatever position you were in when you were saved. I couldn't see the value in this, but it was biblical, so I did. It was 22 years later that I went back to Cliff College as an MA student. That felt strange standing on the same spot where I had thought this was a place I should come to. I hadn't thought about it in the intervening years, but here I was.

The difference I was finding in the Free Methodist church was that the Christians lived and acted like those people in the books I'd been reading. It was getting increasingly difficult to stay at both churches, so I eventually severed my ties with the Methodists and just stuck with the Free Methodists.

That Christmas was my first as a Christian. I went to my first Christmas Eve service. That was so different from every other Christmas – certainly different from the year before when I had been drunk. Christmas suddenly meant something. I also watched *A Christmas Carol* on TV. Alistair Simm was playing Scrooge and when he woke up on Christmas morning after his visits from the ghosts it gave me a really good feeling. He was saved! Dickens may not have seen it like that, but I did. And then there was New Year's Eve. We had a party at the Free Methodist Church – well, it was in someone's house. And when it came to midnight, instead of what had been the obligatory drink, Skip, the minister, prayed us into 1981. That was unusual, but much better.

Another life-changing event soon took place. I met a girl who started coming to the church a year after I had started going. Christmas of 1981 the youth fellowship had a party and I got together with this girl and that was the start of an intense 6 month relationship. I found myself spending more and more time with her because she wanted to see me every hour. She was 3 years younger than me, and she was at school doing A-Levels and I was working. In those days that meant I was seeing a 'schooly' and that was considered perverse. If she had left school at 16 and was working it would have been OK, but these standards were not thought up by deep thinkers. Anyway she had emotional problems as I soon discovered. She had a very bad relationship with her parents and a fear of abandonment. I can remember after one argument with her parents she cried in my arms begging me to never leave her. I was the right person to ask! She also had a morality problem and she tried several times (unsuccessfully) to get me into bed. That was a struggle. I was 19, but I was a Christian. I knew it was wrong, but the temptation was getting beyond me. Then she started acting strange and then she told me it was all over because I was *'too good"* for her. (*'It's not you, it's me'* is what they say these days). That was difficult because I really loved this girl and yet my first emotion when she said that it was over was relief. I needed a break. It had been 7 days a week, every spare moment. But then she turned nasty. She carried on coming to the church for about a year afterwards and she started telling people that I had been seeing another girl in the church (there wasn't a spare minute and this was before mobile phones and the Internet). The reality was that she was seeing her previous boyfriend again and I guess she was feeling guilty.

And then after a couple of months I realised that during my relationship with her I had drifted away from God. And now I felt like what Paul wrote to the Ephesians (2: 12), *'without hope and without God in the world'*. This was unfortunate really because everyone thought I hadn't got over the break-up. I hadn't, and if it had been possible I would have taken her back, but my biggest problem was that I had no awareness of God in my life. I felt lost again. And that was bad because I felt like I had failed God and my girlfriend. I realised that she was not the Christian I thought she was and this was in the days when it was dangerous to go to evangelistic meetings. Let me explain: the evangelist would say at some point in his sermon –*'if you leave this meeting without giving your life to Jesus and you get hit by a bus, where will you spend eternity?'* It always gave me the idea that there were these evangelistic hit-men sitting in buses outside the meetings, revving up their engines ready for those people who weren't saved (as well as those who hadn't changed their underwear – did your mother never tell you that?). Anyway, I thought if she got hit by one of these evangelistic buses she would go to hell and it would be my fault. And that was devastating.

I didn't feel like I could talk to anyone about this – I couldn't tell anyone in the church what we had been doing together, because I didn't want them to judge her. And so I sank into a very black depression. It got to the point where I felt suicidal. I was still reading my Bible every day out of habit – a good habit – but I wasn't praying. I didn't think God would listen to me. I was still going to church. But that was so that people wouldn't ask why I had stopped going. My dad wasn't too happy with me going to church. I was becoming the white sheep of the family and I had been refusing alcohol at family gatherings. If I stopped going he would have considered it good news. Meanwhile for the one and only time, my mum asked me about being a Christian. There I was feeling depressed and suicidal and she said to me one evening, *'What do people mean when they say they have a personal relationship with God?'* I couldn't believe it! I looked up and said, *'Thank you, God!'* and then explained the gospel to her with the help of a '4 Spiritual Laws booklet'. She thanked me and that was it – no commitment.

It was at this time that the Free Methodists were building a church. We had bought some disused barns in a field at the edge of town, just down the hill from where the local witches' coven met. They weren't happy about a church moving in, but read Skip's book for the details.

Every weekend we would work on converting these barns into a church. I remember working on the roof in my suicidal state, rolling out the felt and nailing it to rafters, then accidentally putting my foot through it a couple of times. I used to carry the tiles up the ladder, one in each hand, not holding the ladder, hoping I would fall. I read sometime later that Christian suicides always like to make it look like an accident. I was the same at work as well. I remember that Christmas Eve (1982) climbing a ladder on the roof of a building that was several floors high, hoping I would slip; then there was the time I got so black with despair I attacked my wrist with a screwdriver. Very painful!

The people in my church didn't know how to handle me. Most of them were new Christians and this was a first for them – Christians are not supposed to get depressed. But they did something really good for me. They invited my parents along to church on my 21st birthday (which was a Sunday). I didn't know why they were coming to church for the evening service, but after the service the church had arranged a birthday party for me. That was real Christianity in action. I remember both my parents expressing surprise at how well-liked I was. They didn't expect people to like me!

It didn't take away my depression and it didn't make me cry, (I was depressed – there are no emotions with depression), but it helped. I remember on one occasion we went to hear Eric Delve in Warrington. He was working with *British Youth for Christ* at that time. We were in a church and during the worship time people started singing in tongues and I felt worse and worse the longer it went on. I've never really analysed what was happening before, but it felt like I was being attacked spiritually. It could have been conviction, but I just wanted to get out of there. Eventually it stopped and Eric Delve started preaching. He talked at one point about the idea that each of us is meant to be here. That got me thinking! He said that even if our parents didn't intend us to be born, God did. So, my mind went off again working out, or trying to work out, how God could have arranged for me to be born, given the circumstances of my conception. Did He want *me* – a combination of those two adulterous parents, with all their genetic makeup, or was I to be a combination of my mother and another man? Did God know in advance that I would be born and spend those months in the womb developing those feelings of rejection? How could He not know? How could it be that he arranged for an act of adultery to take place, just to get me here? I spent hours on this one, trying to figure it all out. If anyone can come up with a good answer please let me know. I've heard all the lame inadequate answers.

I honestly cannot remember how I got out of the depression, but I wouldn't be surprised if that dressing table mirror had something to do with it. There was probably another long talk.

This was the beginning of 1983. My apprenticeship had finished on the 4th September 1982 and there were no jobs available. The recession of the 1980s was happening. I didn't want the job, but this was supposed to be my financial security for life. The Unions had arranged with ICI that we all would get to work until the end of April so that we could have experience as tradesmen so that we would stand a better chance of getting another job. My dad still blames me for leaving ICI. He doesn't believe in the recession. He thinks I left the job to hurt him. Some people are more unaware of what is going on around them than I am!

But it was an unnerving feeling knowing that life was stretching out in front of me and I was not qualified, not trained in anything I could actually do, and with no idea what I should be doing with my life.

In some ways that depression was the best thing that could have happened to me. It didn't seem that way at the time, but Romans 8: 28 is actually true, even when it feels as though life is one long, dark tunnel and the only light at the end of it is an oncoming train.

Chapter three

Many are called...

So I applied for Bible Colleges. There was a slight problem with this. Bible Colleges assumed that every Christian who applied was going to be a preacher. I just wanted to go and learn about the Bible. I finally found a college that didn't have preaching as a requirement. It was in Manchester so it wasn't too far from home – I didn't want to lose contact with my church, because there was that problem with separation still. I applied to this college and they didn't reply. Then I applied to CWR for a one week residential course in Christian Counselling. This was in the days before CWR were as successful as they are now and before they bought Waverley Abbey. That course was a life changer. Part of the course involved us breaking into small groups; each group had a staff member in it. In my group we had Selwyn Hughes. I had been reading *Every Day with Jesus* since I became a Christian, so I knew what this man was supposed to be like. He didn't let me down. He told me I should take up counselling full time because he saw the gift in me. I had only just got over my depression. It had been 9 months of darkness and I now had a purpose, a calling, and I was no longer as focussed on my own needs as I was on the needs of other people. At the end of the course Selwyn hugged me. I had never been hugged by a man before and at first it seemed strange, but I've never forgotten it. Acceptance by a well-known Christian leader! I had to feed on his acceptance for a long time afterwards.

I prayed on this course and asked God to direct me. Then when I went home the college had replied to my application, inviting me for an interview. And I passed the interview.

In September 1983 I started as a Bible College student. As with becoming a Christian, I was about to be disillusioned again. I wanted to be at this college: I imagined studying the Bible and Theology with like-minded students in an atmosphere just like church. My naivety eventually left!

So then came the college years, followed by the ministry years! What was life like in a theological college of keen biblical students, desperate to hear from God and looking forward to preparing to serve him?

If you were there you will realise that this is said with tongue in cheek. It was a place of conformity. You had to do what *they* did or you were not living right.

I did like what I was studying. I discovered that I was good at New Testament Greek and I learnt how to interpret the Bible. This is what I had wanted. I had read somewhere that all problems have their roots in Genesis 3 and so I wanted to learn all I could about the Bible, so I could use it to help people.

I also discovered liberal theology. This was an evangelical college: British Isles Nazarene College (BINC), but liberal theology came in to some areas of the teaching. It helped me to understand why those Methodists preached like they did.

But there was also another girl. Well, 3 to be precise. The first girl never did know I liked her. She was a good student and that got her hassle from some of the other girls who were not as committed to working as she was. I never did pluck up the courage to ask her out, but we got on well together and we were friends at college and we are still friends today. I lost touch with her for years and then around the turn of the century I had a strong sense that I should pray for her, so I did. I made enquiries into where she was and after a few months I was given her e-mail address and contacted her in Poland. She was fascinated, because she had been aware of gaining support and guessed that someone was praying for her, but she didn't know who. The second girl I became engaged to. She was an Arab-Israeli from Nazareth.

That was an unintended relationship. I don't remember how it started, but I remember we went to see a Shakespeare play somewhere in Manchester and then we used to walk along the Manchester Ship Canal in the evenings. At some point we decided that this was a genuine relationship, but there were cultural issues. The Arabic way was that we had to get her parents' approval, then get engaged, before we could go out at all. We were a bit late on that, so she wrote to them about me and they approved, so we went to Israel for Christmas, with great plans to get engaged in Bethlehem on Christmas Day. I later learned that I was supposed to buy her for a big bag of gold. I had offended my previous girlfriend when her dad offered to sell her to me for a couple of goats (she was English). I refused and she huffed. So who knows what this one would have said if I'd told her I had no gold.

But Christmas didn't turn out as planned! The parents didn't approve of me. Everywhere I went I found that people didn't approve of me being me! They didn't speak to me in English either, and I wasn't allowed to talk to my girlfriend at all. Her mother told me one morning that I would not be getting their approval and then after 5 days they told me to leave their house! Fortunately I had a friend working in the Nazareth Christian hospital, so I was allowed to ring her and arrange to stay for the night. I was given a lift to the hospital where I 'phoned to change my flight to get back home. I had to leave at 4am the next morning. I took the bus to Jerusalem. I was advised not to get into an Arabic taxi, but there was one taxi driver who kept trying to persuade me to get in with his 3 passengers. This time I felt like there was a sign on my head that said, *English tourist: Please kill me!* I got the bus!

It took me into Jerusalem where I had been assured that all the taxi drivers were safe and they all spoke English. Well, there is an exception to every rule and I got into his taxi. Not a word of English! So I was sitting in the back seat doing an impression of an airplane, showing him my ticket and passport, and off we went – to the wrong airport! I arrived at an inland airport half an hour before my plane was due to take off. Fortunately for me the people on the desk there spoke English and understood my predicament. They 'phoned Ben Gurion airport and told them I was on the way as they called me another taxi. I arrived at the airport to be met by a member of airport security who wanted to know why I was leaving the country early. You've heard of Mossad – Israeli Secret Service; the best secret agents in the world!! I had to get past this man to get home, so I thought a simple racist comment would do it and I told him about my experience with an Arabic family. And with no further questions he let me onto the 'plane 10 minutes after it should have left. I sat in the seat and my head exploded with pain. This was the Christmas from hell!

Four hours later I arrived in England and then National Express wouldn't let me onto the coach back to Manchester because I had a Student Return Ticket and apparently students weren't allowed to return. So I paid the extra with my head still pounding and arrived home. I've never been back to Israel. I'm inclined to agree with God's opinion of the country!

She came back after Christmas to finish her final year at college. We never did define our relationship, but one day she said goodbye and left. I still had the headache! Psychosomatic illnesses like stomach aches and headaches are normal in adopted people and it is likely that as this was another parental rejection that this was the cause. I'm only guessing here because I don't really know, but if you are analysing me as you read this, at least consider it as a possibility.

As the summer holidays were coming up I had a lot of free time, so as I had been invited on a Scripture Union Beach Mission in St. Andrews, Scotland, I went, praying I wouldn't meet anyone else. And that was where I met my wife. She wasn't my wife then of course! I arrived at the church where the team were to meet and made a 'grand entrance'. I could hear voices, but I was in a very dark corridor and I could find neither light switch, nor door handle. Eventually I found the kitchen and could hear the voices through the serving hatch in the wall. So I climbed through the hatch, to everyone's amusement. I met Anne the next day after church.

I could tell this was not going to be a fun fortnight when we were told we had to go to the caravan sites, knocking on the caravan doors to invite any kids to the mission. I hate knocking on doors (even if I know the person I'm calling on), so this was a bad time. Anne rescued me! And then she asked me to help her with a sketch on the beach. She was telling the story of Isaac and Rebekah and she wanted me to play Isaac to her Rebekah. So I did and afterwards we walked through the streets of St. Andrews in our Near-East outfits.

I don't remember much more about that mission apart from hugging Anne as I left. When college started again I asked at the college for Anne's address so I could write to her – she had been a student until two years before I started. It just so happened that my letter arrived on her birthday!

My 2nd year there saw an influx of new and much younger students, many of them straight from school and so not quite as mature as I would have hoped. My most memorable time in this year was when David Jenkins became Bishop of Durham. The understanding seemed to be that God only found out what the Bishop believed after He read it in a national paper. The good Bishop had expressed doubt about the virgin birth and physical resurrection of Jesus. So God had to act fast!

The ceremony had taken place a few months earlier in York Minister, so, slow as a flash, God struck it with lightning, to the delight of the evangelical community. One of the students at college put an article on the college noticeboard explaining how this was God's judgment on the Bishop and on the diocese of York for allowing their Minster to be used. I had recently read an alternative view, so I decided to respond (where angels fear to tread), so I put up my own, handwritten article that said, *'My*

God would have been on time and He wouldn't have missed', with the text Luke 9: 51-56 and my signature at the bottom.

I narrowly escaped crucifixion! It was torn down and I was shouted at and a retraction was demanded. I refused, naturally. And the lecturers all took my side, as did the student who put up the first article and so they both stayed for the next few months, but I was a marked student!

Then there was the cook. She had been off sick for a long time, so she wasn't around in my first year. But now she was back! She was a stereotypical spinster – bitter! And a bully. The kitchen was her domain. And I discovered that my pre-Christian dislike for bullies was still there – I hadn't encountered any since my conversion, but I was now on hallowed ground in Theological College. She didn't like me referring to the college dining room as a canteen, but 'I just couldn't help it'. She made the mealtimes an unpleasant experience and gave me my first experience of bad relations in a Christian context.

Most of my memories of this time are vague. I do remember going to a healing meeting hoping that my daily crippling headaches would be healed. I went forward at the appropriate time as people were having hands laid on them and then falling to the ground. My turn came and the preacher put his hand on my head … and pushed as hard as he could! So I pushed back. I was aware, in front of all these people, that this man was a fraud, as we had this short battle in which he tried to push me over. We called a truce and I went back to my seat.

The next morning I woke up aware that something was wrong. After a few minutes I realised I didn't have a headache – for the first time in 18 months I woke up without a headache. It was the same for the next 5 days, and then on day 6 I woke up with my head exploding in agony. This continued for 3 days and then I woke up without a headache 3 days in a row, but that was it. The headaches were back and remained a daily occurrence for the next 26 years. Explain that one!

This was also the year of Billy Graham's Mission England (Mission Praise really is that old!) and our church was heavily involved in it. We did the Prayer Triplets and the invitations and we hired a bus to go to Liverpool to take any potentials with us. (This was the bus that would hit anyone who didn't make a decision before they left the stadium; although, I don't recall Billy making that threat. But we were ready with our evangelical bus just in case he did, and just in case we could detect anyone who didn't make a decision). Anyway, I invited my dad to come, and he agreed to come!! Not because he wanted to hear Billy Graham; not because he was searching and thought he might find salvation at this mission. He came because his loser son had no one to go with him and so he was doing me a favour! It was a church thing and my 21st birthday had been forgotten, but as I was going and needed to have someone hold my hand, he came. I suppose that was the decent thing, but where did he get the idea that I had no one to go with? Well, as you can guess, Billy (and the Holy Spirit) had no effect on him. He went home no different from he left and we never discussed the event. Well, I tried.

And this was the year I got to know Anne better. She came over to Manchester for a week in the October and then I went to stay at her home just after Christmas. I flew to Belfast on Boxing Day 1984. Christmas was the time the Troubles were at their worst in NI and here I was flying into the country. A friend asked me if I couldn't find a girl from a safe country – last year Palestine, this year Northern Ireland. Anyway, I arrived at Aldergrove International Airport, as it was then, having flown from Speke/Liverpool/John Lennon Memorial Airport. I was met by Anne and her sister. Anne had told her sister that she would recognise me because I would be the scruffiest person getting off the 'plane! And then I met her family – all of them! All together at a Boxing Day party in Comber (no, I didn't know where it was either). Anne's dad drove us home to Armagh in his little red Mini and he decided I should see the Christmas lights in Belfast city centre on the way. I really didn't want to be in Belfast at Christmas, at night, but we survived and then drove into increasing darkness as we drove to pitch blackness.

Anne lived in a tiny village in the middle of nowhere – no traffic, no lights, no nothing. It was known as 'Bandit Country'. This was my introduction to Northern Ireland. I would be back!

So, back to college. There were rules at this college that you wouldn't imagine finding anywhere else. We had to be in bed with lights out by 11pm. I managed to get a weekly late night due to the understanding of the Dean of Students. Every Thursday at 10:30pm "*Hill St. Blues*" was on, and it lasted an hour. So I was allowed to stay in the Common Room till 11:30. And then I brought in the decline of holiness in the college! The thin end of the wedge only has to slip in and before long total corruption reigns. My mum and dad bought a new TV. We must have had the oldest black & white TV in the country, with only 2 channels and one of those knobs you had to click round from the 3 to the 12 position when changing channels – ah, the luxury of remote controls). We still had this TV then a colour one was bought, but this was upgraded. And so now with a black & white in one room and a brand new colour coming to the other room, what was to be done with the old one? Build an extension? Put it in the garage? Well, in a moment of generosity that hasn't been repeated, my dad offered me the TV for our college common room. You just have to know how opposed he is to giving anything to 'the Church'. He is convinced that all churches are financially loaded and ministers are almost millionaires living in mansions (yes he has met me; in case you were wondering). So I checked with the Dean of Students and he was delighted at the offer. And so a Day of Rejoicing was instituted at the college as COLOUR TV arrived. When we went back 4 years later there was a new colour TV and the rules of watching had been dropped – it was even on all day on Sundays. I don't accept all the blame, but I know it was the thin end of the wedge.

I don't remember much else about that year. There was the odd argument in lectures, but generally it was uneventful. And then it was the summer again and so back to Northern Ireland, where I asked Anne to marry me and then I asked her dad if he was OK with that. He didn't ask for a goat, or a bag of gold. I liked that man! Of the 3 fathers-in-law I could have had, he was the best. Even though I couldn't always understand him. He had a bit of an accent!

And so we sailed across the Irish Sea (Larne-Stranraer) to Beach Mission in St. Andrews again and while on the ferry, we got engaged.

And somewhere round about here I decided to leave college. I'd worked out that I would have enough credits by Christmas to get the Diploma in Theology that I had intended, so I decided that I would leave then. I managed to find a live-in job as a "Community Social Worker" as the job was called. It involved living in a Christian half-way house for psychiatric cases who didn't fit anywhere in the system. They were not quite bad enough to be committed, but not quite safe enough to be left alone. This house was in Great Yarmouth. So I worked there practising my counselling skills and my ability to sleep with one eye open – my bedroom door didn't have a lock and these insomniacs tended to like talking at all hours of the day and night. I was there 3 months and then there was to be a big shake up and no more live-in positions. As they were only paying me £30 a week, it wasn't likely that I could rent somewhere, feed myself and work there, so I quit. The one story from that time (for which I have photographic proof) was the night they decided to decorate the whole house. There were about 8 'residents' and on this particular evening I was the only person on duty. I had discovered by this time that Steve was slightly psychotic and Sandra was an arsonist, so when they decided to strip the wallpaper, who was I to stop them? Or should that be *how* was I to stop them? It was OK until the plaster started to come off, at which point they decided that all the plaster should come off – all the walls – in every room!

Anyway, I left in March and on the 5th April I married Anne in Mullaghbrack Parish Church in Co. Armagh. We spent our wedding night in the Inn on the Park and a week later the IRA blew it up. The honeymoon was spent at Spring Harvest in Minehead, Somerset. I was doing counselling after the evening meetings (I know!!!!) We had a blessing service after we got back in the Free Methodist church as the building was now completed.

My family came to this one. My mum and dad had gone to the wedding in Northern Ireland and stayed with my Irish cousins, but no one else would travel over, because they had this strange idea that the IRA went around blowing up weddings. So we had two weddings, complete with dressing up.

And then we lived in a studio flat in Didsbury until October. I had applied to the obligatory 7 universities (in those days it had to be 7) to study Psychology – I was still looking at getting into Counselling. It wasn't as easy back then as it is now. The only university to accept me was the University of Ulster, Jordanstown.

While we were living in Didsbury I read a counselling book and God definitely spoke to me while I was reading and told me I had to become a minister. I told Anne and she was glad I had finally realised something she had known for a while. The problem was that I still couldn't speak in public. Even at our wedding we had to rearrange the reception so that the speeches were done before the meal, so that I would be able to eat.

So I put it to the test. At this point we were going to the Nazarene church in St. Helens. I had transferred my membership from the Free Methodist Church to the Church of the Nazarene because the Nazarenes had a new position – Deacon – which seemed to be what God was calling me to, or so I thought. The St. Helens church was pastored by Tom who had been at college with me. He was still at college, but working part-time. He asked me to preach round about the same time God told me to preach. So I prepared a sermon and prayed desperately. My prayer was for guidance. These were nice people in this church so I wasn't praying for protection against criticism. I prayed that if I had heard God right and this is what I was supposed to do, then I wanted to feel at home in the pulpit. I hated standing up in front of people; I had struggled to do speeches in English at school (I didn't do so well in other languages either); there had been a few times at work when we were supposed to do presentations as part of the apprenticeship and there had been at least one debate I'd had to do at college. I knew I did not feel comfortable talking in front of people. People had told me for years that I would have to get over this fear, but I could never understand why. I was never going to do it.

It was the one thing that I could not face doing. So after praying, I stood in the pulpit, led the service and preached and felt at home. It wasn't the best sermon I've preached. But my prayer was answered and my guidance was given. I wouldn't say my stage fright had gone, but now I knew that I had to face it.

So I went to the college and talked to some of the lecturers. They advised me to abandon university and go back to college to get the extra credits for either the Diploma in Theology and Pastoral Studies – the minimum requirement for ministry – or the Bachelor of Theology.

But I wasn't ready. I thought 3 years in university might be enough time to prepare myself. They told me I could work my way through the next year at college. I had had a grant for the diploma and I was applying to the same education authority for another one for university. The college lecturers told me I didn't stand a chance of getting a 2nd grant. So once again I asked for guidance. I told the lecturers that if God wanted me at the college I wouldn't get a 2nd grant; if He wanted me at university I would get the grant. I got a full grant for the full 3 years. So I went to university.

What a difference! We lived with Anne's sister and her husband. They had bought a big 4 bedroom house in Belfast, so we had part of it converted into a kitchen for us and we had our own facilities. I went into my first lecture, with about 200 students – a lot bigger than the 40 at BINC – and instead of starting the lecture with a prayer, the lecturer told us that now we were at university we should go out, get (drunk) and fornicate. After that, we could study. I could tell that university wasn't going to be like theological college!

Anyway, we started attending a small Nazarene church in South Belfast – Donegall Road Church of the Nazarene. This church was pastored by Raymond who had started college in Anne's last year there and finished college in my first year. I preached once in that church and then I applied for the Nazarene ministry. This involved going before the Selection Panel.

We had to prepare a speech (I did a really bad one) and we had to be interviewed, one to one and then by a panel. They turned me down! They said I obviously wasn't called to the ministry. If I was I would have preached more than twice.

I could see their point, because their view of the ministry was that preaching was the main part of the work. But I knew they were wrong. So I preached a lot more and applied again. This time my speech was more like I would do today – I told them how to ski the Martin Keenan way. I had been on a skiing holiday a few years earlier and I told them all about it. They were very much amused and the comedian I had been in private was now doing stand-up comedy. I was accepted this time, and told that to get into the ministry I had to go back to the college for another year. This was the end of my 3rd year at university. I had switched from Psychology to Sociology by now.

More things happened in the local church before I go on to my return to college. We got involved in the children's work and the first time I reprimanded a boy I was threatened with a knee-capping – he said he would get his dad to do it. I wasn't too comfortable living in Belfast at first. One of my fears growing up had been of living through a war. You need to know where Donegall Road is to realise how dangerous it could be back then.

There was the time I drove one of the old dears home from the Wednesday evening women's meeting and the

IRA were shooting their semi-automatic weapons up the road where she lived. She told me to drop her off and leave in case I got shot. She assured me they wouldn't shoot her. They didn't!

Meanwhile, back with the family, Tamar was born at the end of my first year at university. That was an experience (I'm sure Anne would agree!). I realised two things when I first held her: I had a major responsibility to demonstrate fatherhood to her, so that she would not get any strange ideas about God being a Father; and I realised that this was my first flesh and blood that I knew. This was someone who was mine! That was quite a feeling and it has never gone.

And so she started life in Belfast, going to a church on the peace line. But she liked it there, although now she can't remember it of course.

We had a new minister towards the end of my time at university. Raymond had left and we had a minister imposed on us. He was a bad man! I don't want to say any more because as I said, this is my story and I can't make assumptions about his motives. By the time we left though he had been sacked.

So as I had been told that I had to go back to college, that is what I did. I was not a great Sociology student, so I was glad to be going back to Theology. I decided I might as well do the degree if I was having to do something and so my degree collecting hobby began.

On a family note this year at BINC (which was now

called Nazarene Theological College) was a time of good relations with my parents as we took Tamar to see them and they came to see us fairly regularly. We had one good year!

I had to learn how to preach this year and I had a few interesting trial services. One Manchester church reported that I didn't move when I stood in the pulpit. The content and delivery were not mentioned, but I didn't move enough. Another trial service was in the college church, where most of the lecturers were members. When you've preached to theologians and Bible scholars it's hard to worry about any other congregation. Anyway, they commented on the fact that I didn't shout much (!?) But they liked my sense of humour!

But then I did my 'young preacher's sermon' in the college church and that didn't go down so well. They had changed the standards for entry qualifications for the ministry. From this year there was a distinction made between those who had a degree and those who had a diploma. I didn't think this was a very spiritual approach and argued the point several times. And then came the next trial service in which I compared the college to the church at Laodicea, from Revelation 3. I told them that while they had academic success they were poor, pitiable, blind and naked. The students loved it, but this time I didn't get support from the lecturers. They weren't too happy.

I passed everything, but there was the final report which was given to the District Superintendent and the committee that assessed new ministers before ordination. I wasn't happy with what they had written – there were some factual errors and some lies. Being me I just couldn't accept it, so I asked for a new report. I told the Academic Dean that he should never write anything about someone until he had checked the facts; I pointed out the lies and I wondered what kind of future I would have as a Nazarene minister.

I was given a new report! Not all the changes were made, but I was advised to accept it as it was. So I did. 'They' were still in control!

And then I had to look for a church. There was one available: Donegall Road Church of the Nazarene. The District Superintendent didn't think I would be interested in going back there, so he didn't offer it. But I asked for it and he gave it to me. This was in February 1990; we had to go to the church to talk to the people there about me being their minister. During this final year of theological study the people at the church had sent us money to help us out, and Anne had been praying about where we should go and this fact was highlighted to her during her praying. They had supported us, so we should go and help them.

But before that, I had to go on an assistantship as the final step in my training. This happened in the summer because I didn't get time to fit it in in term-time. It cost £400. I am writing this after 15 years in Methodist ministry and it is fascinating to look at the differences. I went to theological college and paid my own way (with the aid of a grant); anyone training for Methodist ministry is paid. There is no assistantship in Methodist training – ministers are put on probation and are paid right from the beginning. It would be one way of sorting out those who are called from those who are not called.

Anyway, I was sent to Morley in Yorkshire for my assistantship. The reason I was sent was because the minister shouted when he preached and he preached 50 minute sermons. I learnt to preach long sermons, but I still don't shout!

I arrived in Morley railway station on 2nd June and was immediately stopped by a tramp asking me for money. After I had persuaded him of my poverty I was accosted by another tramp.

This was not the easiest introduction to ministry. I received quite a number of criticisms from the minister. The content of my sermons was good, but I wasn't a showman; I wasn't demonstrative enough. He told me on one occasion that I was preaching mind-blowing stuff like I was reading the weather report. There was a compliment in there – did you notice it? There were one or two occasions I really felt like giving up. One thing that kept me going was the support of the congregation.

I actually did some door-to-door work on a housing estate! I got nowhere, but I did it. This was a major event for me.

Part of the process of the assistantship was to send in regular reports to the college. My first report was on the back of a postcard, announcing that I had arrived at the source of the Sacred River Alph (the congregation were all old, it's a literary reference – look it up). Then I sent one telling them I was still an Anabaptist (a theological reference that had to be explained in the college staff room, so very obscure obviously).

Anne and Tamar had gone to Ireland for the summer, they came to see me for a week and when it was ended I flew over to join them and begin life as a minister.

Chapter four

Wars and rumours of wars

So I was now a minister in my first church in Belfast – this church was 37 years old when I went and no minister had lasted in it for more than 3 years. It was a small church and had gone through a troubled time, and for the past year there had been no minister, so a group of people from the Carrickfergus Nazarene church had been looking after it. I started in September and they told me they would be going back to their own church by Christmas. Not a good start.

Well I don't want to change the focus and tell you all about my adventures in Belfast. I will include a few stories to show how I changed as a minister and as a person, because if you are in a non-traditional church with little commitment and you have a problem with rejection you don't have a hope. So, did I have a hope? Well, consider this one: there was a 90 year old woman in this church, who was considered one of our older saints. I went to visit her in my first week there. She obviously didn't remember me, because she talked about the English man who used to go to the church: she thought *he* was supposed to be coming as the minister. Then she told me she was glad it wasn't *him*, because if it was she wouldn't come to church again. I went home after that visit and wondered what to do next.

Just over a month after I started I went to a District Nazarene ministers' meeting where I met Revd. Albert Lown. He was a retired minister from the days of the Cliff Trekkers. He asked which church I was from; I told him, *'Donegall Rd'*; he asked, *'How long have you been there?'*; I said, *'Six weeks'*; he asked, *'And you are still there?'*. It had a bad name!

As did the area where we lived. We decided to get a house in the area round the church. There was no manse and none of the ministers of the other local churches lived in the area, but I thought that as Jesus was incarnational we should copy his method. I don't remember this part of the story, but apparently we went to the Housing Executive to ask for a house and I told them we needed a 3 bedroom house. They asked why 3 of us needed 3 bedrooms, and apparently I told them that there might be a teenage girl who gets pregnant and her parents throw her out of the house and she would need to live with us. So they gave us a 3 bedroom house – there never were any teenage girls living with us, but there could have been!

The house was in what was considered the worst part of Sandy Row – a stone's throw (apparently) from the

Falls Road. When I first saw it, it had windows, but no light fittings, or switches. The place had been gutted. But the Housing Executive fixed it up for us. The only furniture we had was our bed and dining table and chairs – wedding presents. I think Tamar had a bed as well, but that was it. At the Welcome Service they took an offering for us. We bought a good quality carpet for the living room with the money. We really had no chairs to sit on! My study was in the church. We weren't there too long before one of the other Nazarene ministers arranged for a very old, very dusty three piece suite to be delivered. So we had furniture; not a lot of money; we were using Anne's dad's car for the first few weeks and then we were without a car as well. These were the poverty years. But we survived.

I obtained my first dog soon after moving in. I had always wanted a dog, but it wasn't allowed. My dad had a dog when he was growing up, but it died and so he wouldn't have another one.

But there was a woman I met who lived with 7 dogs and much alcohol. Her neighbour was moving and didn't want to take her new puppy with her, so she offered to look after it. She mentioned it to me when I met her and I told her I had always wanted a dog, so one evening I walked home with my new dog on a rope. Anne and Tamar were in the church, so I took the dog in to meet them; it leapt all over them and then messed the church carpet. That was the introduction of Shelly into our family. It was 13 years later that I had to have Shelly put down. That was bad! I told the vet to come to the house and I sat up all night in the kitchen with Shelly, saying goodbye. Six years later Lucky died at the age of 10. We haven't had another dog – they die!

So what do you do when you have a very small church, no confidence and no evangelistic gifts? Panic! Pray!

Our first source of contacts was through the Mother & Toddler Group that Anne had started when we were previously in the church – it was still running. By January we had started a Playgroup, sponsored by Social Services. This was in the days before Ofsted and when Playgroups were not part of the educational system.

I got to know a lot of the locals through living in the area. I developed a friendship with someone who came from outside, but had a lot of contacts. Every time anything happened – shootings, bombings, etc. I would go and see him and he would give me the details. I was well-informed about the Troubles.

Evangelistically I wasn't seeing much success but my stage fright was rapidly vanishing. There are a lot of stories from this time that I use as sermon illustrations, but they don't detail anything about how I was managing as a minister. I always felt I was in the right place, doing what God wanted me to do, but I was never convinced I was that good at it. I always hoped for a revival to end the Troubles, but it didn't happen. It was here though that I developed the idea of a church for the unwanted. This is where most of my contacts came in. There were young couples who had babies, but because they were not married the other churches wouldn't 'christen' their kids. One couple came to me and I offered a Thanksgiving Service. From then on I had a lot of contacts among these unchurched young families. I developed my ability to preach the gospel without fear. We had the kind of church where the morning service was for the Christians and the evening service was supposed to be a gospel meeting – even if the same people came to both. I remember after my first evening, preaching on John 3: 16, wondering what was left to say. After a year or two I closed the evening service and we concentrated everything in the morning.

My old attitudes of not being pushed around came out again in this church, hopefully in a sanctified way. We were getting grants for developing our church land as a playground, when the neighbouring Church of Ireland Select Vestry came round to see me in force, telling me I had to let them share the playground, or else. There were 5 or 6 of these big men in my church making demands, and I threw them out. I realised that turning the other cheek is for personal affronts, not for when others are threatened. Although when our window was broken and I chased after the kids I assumed were responsible (I chased them in my car) that was personal. When it was blamed on the son of the local UDA commander (allegedly) I went to his house and demanded payment. Not the wisest move, but I was mad at this point. The glazier came back to fit the window and told me he had overestimated the cost of the window, which mistake I think may have been caused by my 'pastoral' visit. Maybe he paid for part of it – I never asked. But that UDA man wouldn't speak to me for months afterwards. Everyone told me I should be grateful my kneecaps were still working, but that was the authority of the ministry in a place like that. When the 6 year old son of another local UDA men was killed in a freak car accident outside his own house I became very popular and this first man started speaking to me again – it was a son of his friend and I visited a lot. A week later he was in hospital with a bullet hole in his chest, with the exit wound in his lower back. We had an interesting hospital visit. It was quite a place. He had been shot in our local pub. We had moved house to Roden Street at this point and I was intending to go to the pub on the Saturday before Christmas to invite all the locals to our Christmas services. I changed my mind and went on the Friday instead. Blame God for this one, because on the Saturday the INLA kicked in the new security door, sprayed the place with bullets, killing 3 and injuring everyone else. I went the day before I intended to go!

But there was still the assessment of ministry to contend with. The system in the Nazarene church was that a minister was given a licence for a year and then interviewed near the end of the year, each year, to test his or her call. In the year of the 4th licence (i.e. 3 years after the 1st one) it was ordination time if everything went well. Ordination happened at the District Assembly, which was normally in Paisley, Scotland. The year of my ordination (1993) it was in Belfast. My parents decided to come, surprisingly. I remember going for a walk with my dad on the afternoon of my ordination; he asked me why I was doing this as I could not speak in public and I didn't get on with people. He gave me 6 months before I would quit. He didn't seem to realise I had been in the ministry for two and a half years at that point, preaching twice every Sunday. He still wasn't aware of what was going on – but then if he knew where we lived he wouldn't have come to stay with us and he certainly wouldn't have gone for that walk. He just didn't seem to realise how dangerous a place it was, but ignorance can be bliss and he didn't get shot.

Later on in that year we had a mission. Again in the Nazarene church it was required that each church organise an evangelistic mission each year, but this is the only one I want to write about. Graham Lawther had written a book: *A very long way from Paradise*; his life story. Graham had grown up in the Village – an area of Donegall Road that wasn't particularly safe. He had been arrested for possession of a gun and in prison he was saved and he became an evangelist. He had taken several missions in Belfast – very successful. His book was producing converts as people read it. And then he got in touch with me and I asked him to do a mission in the Village. His method was that he spent a week knocking on doors, talking to people and offering a copy of his book, followed by a one night meeting on which he would preach. This had been successful up to now. In the Village he received death threats and the threat that if he held a meeting certain people would fire guns into the place. So we arranged with the City Mission in the Village to use their mission hall. I led the meeting and Graham spoke; on the front row were a few of Graham's friends who had offered their help/support/protection. They were converted Loyalist terrorists, muscular, tough looking, dressed in black leather jackets and jeans. I stood at the front with the front door directly opposite me, thinking, *If anyone bursts into here, I'm right in the firing line, literally*, but they had been idle threats. We had one convert. It was the hardest area Graham had worked in and the least fruitful. He was an evangelist; imagine what it was like for me!

I have never had a mission since that was anything like that one. Sometime round this I did a Youth Mission for the Lisburn Church of the Nazarene. This time I was the evangelist. This was a new experience for me: I did open-air preaching; I had a Christian rock group as a support act, with me as the main feature. I preached in the Lisburn Nazarene church for the first (and last) time on the Sunday. When I began my Bible reading 5 people stood up and walked out. I was reading from the Revised Standard Version – a compromise on my part because I usually read from the New International Version, but Lisburn was dominated by a spirit of legalism and only the King James Version was allowed. But 5 kids were saved, so that made up for it; it also made up for the anonymous letters I received in the post afterwards, warning me that I was heading for hell for not using the Authorised Bible.

It was also around this time, after we had moved to Roden Street that we found ourselves in the eye of the storm, or the centre of a massive Loyalist riot. There had been a terrorist's funeral in Shankill Road and the police had not allowed a paramilitary show, so all the Loyalist areas in Belfast decided to riot, in protest. At the bottom of Roden Street there was a big pile of wooden pallets, prepared for the 12th July bonfire. The riot happened on a Saturday night. I have to admit that I wasn't aware of it; all I was aware of was what I saw on Sunday morning. Our car was sitting outside our house – the only car on the street. The wooden pallets had been dragged across the road and were still smouldering; at the top of the street was a fire engine, lying on its side, still burning. The fire engine had been called out to put out the fire on the bus, which was on the other side of the street, also lying on its side, on fire still. As we walked to church along Donegall Road we saw the burnt-out remains of (as we were told later) 26 cars that had been set on fire. Our car was untouched!

Tamar started school while we were still living in Sandy Row. The local school was across the road from our house, but it wasn't producing good results, as our Sunday school kids demonstrated, so we decided she wasn't going there. There was a school on Donegall Road, so we made an appointment there and were equally not impressed, although they told us that one of their former pupils had eventually gone to Oxford!. Then there was the day I was walking down the Lisburn Road in Belfast, just outside our area and I happened to notice Fullerton House Preparatory School – the Prep. School for Methodist College – so I walked in and asked to see the principal. He saw me, without appointment and I asked him what was so good about his school that they charged for it. (Ignorance is still bliss!)

Tamar had an interview and spent three happy years at school. Anne took her in the first day and she was fine. I took her in the next day and she clung to my neck crying that she didn't want to go. That was difficult – memories of parental separation came flooding back. I unpeeled her from my neck very reluctantly and the teacher took her in her arms and I had to turn to go (with tears in my eyes, never mind Tamar's). I reached the school gate when one of the other parents came running over to tell me that Tamar had stopped crying and was quite happy!

After 4 years we decided to leave. There are reasons for this that I won't put in print, but it was from this point on that we decided never to trust Social Services again.

So we left, on the 30th August 1994. The next day the IRA called their ceasefire. I'm sure the two events were unrelated.

We moved to Taunton in Somerset.

Chapter five

Things can only get better!

But before we moved to Taunton I have to say a few
things about what happened shortly before the move.
The church in Belfast grew and then shrank and I had to
wonder what I was doing right and what I was doing
wrong. The Nazarene church unofficially seems to blame
the minister for a church's failure to grow, so it does
involve a lot of introspection, although, as a holiness
church, it considers introspection to be carnal. We bless
God when the church grows – officially. We blame the
minister if it doesn't grow – unofficially. And so I left
wondering if I had anything to offer to this new church.
I didn't go there brimming with confidence, but then I
never go anywhere brimming with confidence. I just trust
God that He knows what He's doing.

But the really weird thing that I cannot leave out was
the nightmares. I had three while still in Belfast. I've
never had any doubts about the supernatural and I've
never doubted the location of the Twilight Zone (it's in
here somewhere), but these nightmares were something

else. Because I'm being honest I mention the three, but I can only remember the first one and the third one. These were the most vivid, demonic, nightmares I have ever had. I have had weird dreams and nightmares, but nothing like these. I was fighting a demon on the stairs of our house in the first one. I won because I called out the name Jesus and woke up. In the third one I was running down the street in which we lived, being chased by a herd/flock/gaggle(?) of demons and I suddenly thought, *'Why am I running?'* so I shouted, *'Jesus! Jesus! Jesus!'* and woke up. To any Freudians out there: analyse that! If you think that was weird wait until I write about the ghost I saw a few years later – I don't believe in ghosts, but I saw one!

And so to Taunton. This was definitely God. This church was 11 years old when we went to it. It had been started in Taunton itself, but then a grotty little Congregational church building was for sale on the edge of town and being a fairly traditional church the Nazarenes decided to buy it, even though there were very few houses near this building – and they couldn't afford it! In their 11 years they had had 4 ministers, one of whom had been responsible for splitting the church, which resulted in all the younger people leaving and forming their own church and it had now been 2 years since their last minister had left. They had bought a manse next door to the church and the mortgage was being paid by the rent that the tenants were paying. I asked for a move and Taunton asked for a minister, in the same week. They took it as a sign and so it probably was. This was a new church and so the people running it were new Christians and they were not that organised. There were two major personalities in the church who each thought that they were running things, so there were issues when we first arrived. One major issue that affected us was that the church ran out of money two weeks after we arrived! As we were living in the manse there was no more rent coming in and there was a mortgage and a minister to pay – I was on a pay rise now- £100 per week. The Nazarene District were reluctant to help financially – they thought I should be able to grow the church quick enough to fund the church. But they eventually helped out. I don't remember too much of the first year in Taunton. I remember I started knocking on the doors in the area. We lived in a grotty manse in need of much repair and there were new houses being built all around us, so as soon as a Sold sign went up I would be knocking on the door inviting people to church. I kept that up until we left.

Tamar's schooling was a problem again as State education isn't brilliant, but we put her in Taunton Prep School after the first half-term (paid for by Anne's dad {as in Belfast} and a good bursary).

By the second year the church could not afford me at all, so I started looking around for other Nazarene churches to see if I could move. There were none available. So I started to look for jobs. Anne was working as a TA in the local secondary school, but we didn't have much money. All I could find was voluntary work, so I took that with the idea that when I had experience maybe I could get a paid position. My voluntary work was with Turning Point, one of the national Drug and Alcohol agencies. I became a drug worker! I had a lot of training from them, learning about HIV/AIDs and addiction and drugs in general. Having been a Christian for 15 years this was a completely different environment for me. In Belfast I had been the minister working in the Troubles, but here I was a drug worker. I saw a lot of problem lives and difficulties and it showed me that we have to offer more than a church service with guitars and soft chairs to help people like these.

Anyway it was round about this time that I ran into a Nazarene minister who was also working as a double-glazing salesman (you couldn't make this up!). He was looking at grants to get our church building double glazed and he told me that he was considering transferring to the Methodist ministry. He suggested that I should consider it. I laughed! I had experienced the Methodist church when I first became a Christian and I didn't want to have anything to do with Methodists again. But occasionally I can be open-minded and so my former youth club leader got me a subscription to the Methodist Recorder and so I started reading it – every week (honestly! For a year!) There were evangelicals in the Methodist church and they were starting to become more prominent and so I started to pray about this. We even attended a few Methodist church services in town – and they were so boring!

But I applied anyway. This was a big risk because they ask for a reference from your current church, which meant telling the Nazarenes that I was considering leaving. If I wasn't accepted they wouldn't be happy with me staying. But at this point they weren't paying me. I was signing on and working for nothing, so they couldn't really complain.

Part of the process involved having a psychological evaluation. I had never had one of these before, so this was not something I was looking forward to. I had to go to Exeter to meet with a psychologist. As I was leaving Anne said to me, '*If he asks about your childhood, lie! If you tell him the truth they'll never accept you*'. He asked me about my childhood! I assumed Anne was joking, so I told him an edited version and he said, '*Have you ever considered seeing a psychiatrist?*' Honestly! He said that! So I replied, '*Have you ever considered the gospel of Jesus Christ?*' God had to be in it, because I can't imagine what he wrote about me in his psychological assessment.

The interviews were in London in May 1996, so we made a day of it and we all went to London – to Methodist Church House on Marylebone Road (just like in Monopoly!) This means I was accepted for interview; there were over 200 applicants that year from other

80

denominations. There were about 20 of us for the interviews. The train fare to London was £64 and the Methodist church said they would reimburse it, but the coach was £11 and we thought that made more sense – they were only going to reimburse me. But it was the first day of the Chelsea Flower Show and so because of the traffic I turned up 45 minutes late for my interview.

They had assumed I had changed my mind, but as there were one-to-one interviews, and panels, and small group interviews I was able to have my one-to-one interview walking around Regent's Park. My prayer all along had been that if this was not right I wanted them to turn me down. I only prayed negatively about this. There wasn't an evangelical on the interview panel at all and I answered the questions I was asked as honestly as I would today and then the day ended and we took the coach back home. Not long after we arrived home Methodist Church House 'phoned me to say I had been accepted! They wanted me to go back a month later for another meeting with them, and this time they insisted that I took the train!

And so back to London it was – to learn how to conduct Communion services! We were told that communion is all done by the book, and it was important to know where to stand when doing which bit – it was a few months later when I heard that one 'presided at communion' with black shoes. Any other colour was theologically incorrect. The things you don't learn from the Bible and studying theology in an evangelical college! Eternal issues like brown or black shoes and we were not even told! To think, if I hadn't transferred into the Methodist ministry, what Judgment Day would have been like for me. Jesus would be saying: '*I told you to do this to remember me! Do you not remember I was wearing black shoes when I said it?*' Fortunately for me I obtained forgiveness. But then there were the cassocks and gowns and stoles, and I nearly believed them!

It got worse! I discovered the Interfaith Movement on one of these training occasions. These people believed that all religions lead to God – Jesus is just optional. I nearly walked out when I heard that one. I did walk out when I went into a room for a 'time of worship' and found Buddhas and Muslim icons set out for us to contemplate. I was ready for tearing my hair out. And then to be told that homosexuality was a preference, not a sin and my understanding of the Bible was inadequate! That is typical of liberals – they have no good theological arguments, so they resort to insults.

By this time I knew that I was being sent to a rural circuit in North Yorkshire, so I asked the man who was to be my District Chairman what I was likely to find there and he assured me they were evangelical and so would think like me. He was half right!

And so we went to Sherburn (I have to say it was the other Sherburn, because there are two in North Yorkshire and everyone who has heard of them always assumes it was Sherburn-in-Elmet. It wasn't!) There were 9 churches; I was the only minister; I was put on probation for 2 years (bad choice of word!) as an ordained probationer. If I had transferred in from the Church of England I would not have been on probation, but as a mere Nazarene I was not good enough to get straight in. I say this because at the moment the Methodists are complaining that the Church of England does not recognise Methodist ordination.

I was given a piece of paper allowing me to conduct communion services in my own churches. I thought that was insulting so I tore it up.

Those first two years were difficult! Who am I kidding? Those first 5 years were difficult. I have never had so much trouble in my life as I had in those first 5 years in Methodist ministry. Every day I thought they would sack me for the unforgivable sin of being me, but somehow I'm still here! I said God wanted me here and He wins!

So where to begin? My first trouble I suppose. I had never experienced circuit stewards before and I had three classic stewards here. Let me just say here that for some deep Freudian psychological reason Anne could never get used to calling it a circuit and so she kept referring to it as a circus. Well if these were circus stewards, that makes them a bunch of clowns and that's about right. My first holiday was around Christmas and as these three circuit stewards were always bickering with each other I decided that I would record a message on my answering machine that told anyone with a problem to contact the circuit treasurer. For some reason, the only female steward phoned the manse while I was away and she contacted Diotrephes, one of the other two. Diotrephes was about 6 feet tall and a cross between Larry Grayson and Dale Winton. Well, when we got back we were in Diotrephes' church for the first Sunday service and after the service he summoned me for a word. He liked to tower over people, so I made him sit down and then he asked who I thought I was leaving a message like that on my machine. I said, '*Did you expect me to put your name on my machine? What if it had been a pastoral emergency? When you can learn to get on with people…*' And I left him sitting there fuming.

Well one good thing was that the people liked my preaching. I had been regarded as a good preacher in the Nazarene church, and here in the Methodist church I was recognised as being good. I'm not boasting here: this is the gift God gave me and so it's his gift, so I'm not going to run it down in a fit of false humility.

But I was on probation and that meant trial services. This was where I was criticised badly. Apparently I can't preach and once again my understanding of the Bible is inadequate. This was the opinion of my District Chairman. I'd already heard him preach once and so I didn't let his opinion affect me too much – he couldn't preach at all! And then we went to Easter People – what was described as Spring Harvest for Geriatrics – it was our one and only time. When we returned I had a letter, and I have to say that I have hated opening letters since this one. There had been complaints about me. I had preached on Easter Sunday and two couples in that particular church had written to complain. This was my first experience of the Methodist Complaints procedure (there was a second to come a few years later) and this stage involved me having a meeting with the church stewards of that church, with the District Chairman and with the two couples. I have taken on UDA terrorists so I know what threatening situations are like and I'm not scared of people, but I had never experienced anything like this before. What was my crime? I had said, on Easter Sunday morning, in the sermon, that Jesus died. Well bring on the Spanish Inquisition! I was told that it was completely inexcusable to say that on Easter Sunday morning. I was supposed to preach about his resurrection. So, naturally, I asked, 'Resurrection from what?' Me, I would have laughed at that, but they just turned purple. I was accused of 'smirking' in the pulpit. I thought it was a smile but that's me. Apparently smiling was not acceptable either. I had been required to send my sermon notes to the District Chairman and he said, at this meeting, that normally he takes the side of his ministers, but on this occasion he couldn't. I was accused of preaching for 20 minutes. Now you have to believe this next bit. I was being genuine. I thought the complaint was that I didn't preach for long enough – my sermons had been 30 minutes in the Nazarene church, so I responded, '*I preach for 25 minutes*'. I know, but give me a break I was new to this established church stuff.

But that wasn't the end of it. One of my accusers said I had started my sermon by saying, '*My favourite thing about Easter is blood*'. I immediately protested that and said, '*My favourite thing about Easter is chocolate!*' Not a twitch of a smile. One of my other accusers got so frustrated that he stormed out and the whole thing left a bad taste.

I wasn't happy with the whole affair, but the good side of it was that a lot of supportive letters were written from the circuit to the District Chairman – he never acknowledged them.

And then a few months later I had to have my first District meeting as a 'probationer' to see how I had managed. Did they want to know how I had managed? Did they want to know how I had settled into Methodism? Not at all. The whole panel had been given a copy of my sermon notes and that is all they wanted to talk about.

One self-satisfied, smug member of the panel asked me if I was a Good Friday Christian or an Easter Sunday Christian. I just looked at him and he misinterpreted my look and started to explain what he meant, so I interrupted him with, '*I'm a Pentecost Christian!*' End of conversation.

I was just about recommended to be accepted for a second year of probation. I was marked as 'Adequate'. I had to think back to my tendency to see everything in terms of rejection, but it just wouldn't kick in. I started to think seriously that I was in the wrong place. Up until that point I had been a good minister and a good preacher, but now I was adequate. That's the lowest they can give anyone. I've never heard of anyone else getting such a bad recommendation.

But I survived. And did it get better? Not a chance. My next memory is the church council meeting in that same church. There was a Mother & Toddler Group that met every Thursday in that church – 90 families. Imagine that! There really were 90. I'm not exaggerating the figures so you will be impressed. There really were 90. But none of them came to church. So in this church council meeting the church member who ran the group gave a report and Diotrephes said we should stop allowing the group to meet in the church unless they started to come to church on a Sunday morning. There were a few murmurs of agreement and this group leader left in tears. And I lost it – the first time since I became a Christian! I couldn't believe that this was a Christian church; I couldn't believe what was being done in the name of Jesus Christ. And so I told them, loudly. I told them they were a disgrace and they should be ashamed of themselves and that they should resign from church membership.

This was the church that my predecessor was scared of and I had been warned about. The funny thing is that my first example of bad behaviour occurred in one of the other churches a week earlier. I had so many churches and I got the time wrong on this church council meeting. It was to start at 7pm and I arrived at 7: 15pm. By this time the secretary had been having a little disagreement with one of the members – a local preacher on trial. I prayed to officially start the meeting and then these two men started up again, until the local preacher stood up and stormed out. So I turned to the secretary and said, '*OK, now what do we do?*'

What was I doing in a church like this? I was convinced that God had a plan and I'm glad He hadn't given me those details beforehand. I really just want a quiet life!

Anyway, the first positive – there had to be one – came in this second church I mentioned. They had been running Alpha courses for a couple of years by this stage. I had a 'phone call one evening asking if I would come to the 'Healing night' of their Alpha course. I was the minister, I was told, so I would know what to do!

I had never been on an Alpha course before, so I had no idea what it was about. This circuit had a group that met most Sunday evenings where they had prayer afterwards and people would fall down – this was before the Toronto Blessing. So I went to this Alpha night – no meal! I watched the video and then it was assumed I would lay hands on and pray for anyone who had a condition that needed healing. You can imagine I had no great expectations, but I laid hands on a couple of people and they were healed.

I was fascinated! I know God heals, but it had never happened through me before. So the circuit wanted me to run Alpha courses from then on. I agreed on condition they pay me to go to a training session at Holy Trinity, Brompton. So off to London I went, to see Nicky Gumbel in action.

This was getting more like it. I laid hands on people and they dropped to the ground. We had a few people saved, but nothing major.

And then trouble flared up again. It was near the end of my first year and I had taken another few days off. We had a meeting in that circuit that they called the 'pre-circuit meeting'. It is really called the 'Circuit Leadership Team meeting', but that is what they called it. It was held in the manse, with the circuit stewards, the circuit treasurer and the circuit meeting secretary. It became obvious that there had been an earlier, unofficial meeting, because after we had planned the circuit meeting agenda the secretary was asked to leave, and I thought, '*Here we go again*'. The circuit treasurer was the spokesman and he said that I had been out of the circuit without informing them, and that wasn't acceptable. He said that if was to leave the circuit again I had to announce the fact in the circuit newsletter. I really wasn't sure what these people were used to, but I knew what I wasn't used to and it was being spoken to like that. So I told the treasurer (who lived in a big house surrounded by his own 9 hole golf course, in a little country village), that if he would take out an advertisement in the local paper next time he was on holiday, then I would advertise my home as being empty. Funnily enough I didn't get any more hassle from them after that.

Chapter six

And so it ends

This seems an appropriate place to have a look back. The purpose in writing this is not to tell everything that happened in my life. It is to look at the underlying theme of rejection and how to overcome it with God in your life. That's not how it began, but it is how it feels on this side of the keyboard. So I have to say that the Church of the Nazarene did not ever reject me. They turned me down for the ministry the first time I applied, but they did not reject me as a person. And so the next time I applied they accepted me and throughout my 6 years with them they did not reject me as a person.

The Methodist Church was different. On one of those early meetings I mentioned, before moving to my first circuit, I was told by a member of the team training us that I would never fit into the Methodist Church; I would never belong; I would never be one of them. The Methodist Church is for Methodists, I was told by this representative of the Methodist Church. Now I couldn't take that personally because she was speaking about her own inadequacies and she did not know me, but still, it sounded very familiar. But I could take personally the report on me at the end of my second and final year on Probation. Diotrephes was now no longer a circuit steward and his replacement was much better, but the report was not good – again. Did they want to know about the healings, or the people who had been saved, including a group of teenagers, resulting in a new Sunday school being started? No, they wanted to attack my personality. Now, I'm not paranoid, but even if I am, it seemed as though they really were out to get me.

The report claimed that the circuit stewards had said that I was '*shy*'. I hadn't been accused of that since childhood and even then it wasn't true. I withdrew into my own world and I exhibited passive aggressive tendencies, but I wasn't shy. Anyway, I asked each of the circuit stewards if they had actually said this about me; and they hadn't! It was a set up! So I told the District Chairman that there was some doubt about the honesty of his report. (It was Yorkshire and I am me, so it was less flowery than that sounds!) There was no response until I got to the interview where the District Chairman said, '*I believe you are not happy with your report*'. So I said, '*Well it's not true. You made it up*'. But it was me against all of them and even though I protested that he had made this stuff up about me, they took his side and the report officially went out that I didn't have the right personality to be a minister in the Methodist church. I had been a minister for 8 years at this point.

You can imagine I wasn't feeling too welcomed by this denomination at this point. It was not easy moving on from there, but they did just about accept me and so I was to be 'Received into Full Connexion'. The Methodist Conference that year was in Scarborough, so it was easy travelling. I couldn't guarantee I would have travelled to it if it had been much further away, but I sat through what felt like a meaningless service – the only meaning it had was that now they couldn't touch me. The only 'offences' they could get me on now was rebaptising someone who had been 'done' as a baby and refusing to baptise the child of a Methodist member.

But did I want to stay? Well, obviously not. I had never met such an unwelcoming, unfriendly church.

There were a few more events before I left this first circuit. I was only allowed to stay 5 years. The first event was the death of one of my church members: Jenny was 60 years old and she had asthma. She died of a heart attack during an asthmatic attack and that got me thinking that my natural (biological) mother might be dead, so I decided to do what I had always said I would never do. I contacted Social Services and asked for my birth records. The rule was that an interview had to take place with a social worker to make sure I wasn't mentally deranged – I passed! She also told me that there is a record of birthmothers who would like to contact their children. Mine had not registered. There was no surprise there. I would have been stunned if I discovered that she had been looking for me. When I met her she told me that she hadn't heard that this was possible. I would have thought the mother-baby bond was strong enough that mother would do all she could, but like I say – no surprises!

Then the social worker gave me the details of my birth so I could send for my birth certificate. I was pleased to discover that my birthday was right all along – I have recently heard of someone who was given the wrong date. I wasn't keen on the original name I had been given and I was amused at "*Saint Monica's Home for Unmarried Mothers*" as my birth place. It sounds like something out of a Dickens story. My mother worked as a '*Boot and shoe operative: leather uppers*' – I come from high society! Leather uppers!

She wasn't a secretary as I had been told and she didn't live at home with her parents – everything I had been told about myself was false!

So, we were in Yorkshire and Cumbria was only on the other side of the country and we started taking trips across there to look through the records and get the necessary certificates. I found my mother's birth certificate – and that is how we discovered the details mentioned at the beginning.

But I didn't want to meet her. She was the first rejecter! I remember looking at my daughter when she was 8 weeks old and wondering how anyone could give their child away at this age (or any age), so I didn't want to meet the mother who had given me away. To be rejected by a parent once may be regarded as a misfortune. To be rejected by the same parent twice looks like carelessness – as Oscar Wilde would have said.

We went to the little village she grew up in, and at the school she probably attended; we even went to the church where she was married a year after I was born. And we found her current address. But that was as far as it went for now.

The other significant event at this time was when I went on a one year part time Christian Counselling Certificate course. That was an achievement I was pleased with, but as it meant driving to Birmingham once a month I developed a pain in my leg. I thought it was caused by the driving, but when it didn't go away after two years I went to see the doctor. He took some blood tests and a couple of days later, when the results came in, he rang me in a panic and insisted that I go to see him as soon as possible.

So I did – as you would! He told me I was severely anaemic (8.5 for those with any medical understanding – 'very bad' for those without). He asked me if I was tired. I said: I've got 9 churches, who wouldn't be tired. So it was hospital visits for a variety of tests and things poked inside me and the result was *coeliac disease*. The lining of my small intestine was stripped; I had osteopenia (the beginnings of osteoporosis, caused by my inability to absorb calcium, and everything else), so I immediately had to go on a gluten-free diet. No more biscuits and cakes! I was devastated. This condition is also associated with diabetes and I was praying hard that I could at least keep chocolate – I could. And so I had to take up weight-bearing exercises as well. And the results were good. I gained a stone in weight and none of my clothes fitted because I suddenly developed the normal amount of muscle (well, you should have seen me before!)

Other things happened, but before we leave this first Methodist Circuit I only have one more event to mention – it seems appropriate to end on a positive: the circuit organised a farewell evening for us. It was to be held in Sherburn's church hall, so as it was a short walk (quarter of a mile) down the village, we decided to walk to it. As soon as we got out of our cul-de-sac we could see cars parked everywhere. I thought there must have been something on in the village hall, because the whole village was lined with cars on both sides of the road, (I didn't say I'd learned anything did I!). So we arrived at the church hall and found it packed with people. Now that was acceptance! They had put on all kinds of sketches and songs; they even brought in a choir (OK, they didn't know me that well!) and I was stunned. It was nice, as I was leaving, to hear how much I was appreciated – there were speeches too.

But before I leave Yorkshire I have to mention that ghost that I promised a while back. It was 2am, or thereabouts and I had woken up. Our house had a long corridor upstairs. Tamar's bedroom was at the top of the stairs and our bedroom was at the other end of this corridor, with the bathroom next to it. I got up to go to the bathroom and I was wide awake. I came out of the bathroom and looked down the corridor and there is this woman in a white, flouncy Victorian-style dress, holding a lantern, and she had a really demonic face, glaring at me. She was gliding down the corridor towards me. It was an interesting time with all kinds of healings and things and I just looked at this 'ghost' and said, '*Oh go away, I don't believe in ghosts*', turned my back on it and went back to bed. I'm assuming it left sulking, because it never came back.

This may sound weird, and my reaction may not seem normal, but it was just how things were back then. I can't guarantee I would react the same now, but then I don't expect to see any more ghosts – I don't believe in them. Although I am very aware of the spiritual forces of evil in the heavenly realms. I would hate to live in a materialistic atheist world – it would be so boring.

And so we moved to Hailsham in East Sussex, to take over the Hailsham Methodist church and to start 'The church at the Haven School', a church for unchurched people. This involved going through the stationing process, which began the November before.

The process, at that time, involved choosing 10 circuits, having read the profiles of about 200 or more that were looking for a minister. I struggled to find any, but eventually I sent them off and they were ignored! No surprises there! But you can't beat God. I had a 'phone call telling me I had been matched with the Douglas & Peel circuit on the Isle of Man. I hadn't put them on my list and they hadn't put me on theirs, but the District Chairman had transferred in from the Salvation Army and he saw my Church of the Nazarene background and thought I would be good for the dying Manx Methodists. They didn't agree. They flew us over in December, to stay in the best hotel in Douglas. There was one evangelical and he was the only friendly person we met. If I thought I had met hostile, unfriendly Methodists before, well... One of them even argued with me over what was allowed on my gluten-free diet. The superintendent minister was not happy that I hadn't been brought up a Methodist – seems that woman was right about not being accepted. And so they turned me down. I have never been back to the Isle of Man and nothing would persuade me to go. When I was looking for where to go 10 years later my District Chair (they were no longer chair *men*) sent me a text saying, '*How do you feel about the Isle of Man?*' I replied, '*I hope you are joking*'. He texted back, '*No. Why?*' I replied, '*I'll tell you later*'. The Isle of Man had been 4 circuits, it was now down to 1 and they had read about the Haven church and thought I would be good for them – they left it too late!

So I had to look at what was left on my list and none of my choices were there so I had to choose from the leftovers. I don't remember what was at the top of my list, but Eastbourne circuit was second and I was matched up with them. They hadn't put me on their list because they thought North Yorkshire was so far away that we wouldn't move. They accepted me instantly. I asked if I could meet the people with whom I would be planting the church and they said, '*No, they are not a church, so they can't make a decision*'. Did you know that the name 'Methodist' originally was an insult because they were so methodical? I wonder if we could rename the denomination on the basis of how they do things today! I could come up with some names!

Anyway, we drove home and they rang to tell us they wanted us to come, so I asked then if I could meet the 'church planting team' and so the circuit paid for me to go down a second time. I went alone this time. I met the team and when I got back home, I said to Anne: '*This church plant will never work with those people*'. And I wasn't wrong!

Chapter seven

And as I face the final curtain

It did work – but not with those people. We planted and grew a church of mostly unchurched young adults with kids running round everywhere. We had a youth club for the local area with 50 teenagers attending regularly. A lot of what happened in the planting of the Haven is recorded in other places and doesn't fit into my life story. It has appeared in the Methodist Recorder, Headline magazine and I wrote an *MA in Evangelism Studies* dissertation on the subject.

But I wouldn't do it without help so I went on the Methodist Church Planting Course and met some Methodist evangelicals; I read books on church planting and new forms of evangelism; I joined Willow Creek Association UK. I was looking for help wherever I could find it.

The Hailsham church had some interesting characters, but by this stage they couldn't touch me. I had become immune to Methodist insults. I remember, a few years in, when the Haven was going well and one member at Hailsham who liked to put on Christingle services asked me to lead the service. She said, *'We don't want you to preach, because there will be unchurched people coming and we don't want you to put them off'*. I just laughed, because this woman had no idea who Jesus is and she only heard of unchurched people from me and she was trying to be offensive. But the Haven was working, so they really couldn't touch me. There had come a time when I asked for a 'curtailment' – Methodist-speak for 'I want to leave now!' It was granted, but the local Anglican Bishop asked me to stay. I said I would, but there were 3 conditions. He fulfilled the conditions: we moved into the Anglican vicarage in Eastbourne, I was sole minister of the Haven and I was no longer responsible for Hailsham. Most of the Haven congregation left as well, but that was no bad thing – we started again. Five years later the same Bishop wanted me out and so although the church gave me a 100% recall, the circuit gave me a 71% vote and I needed 75%, so I had to move, very reluctantly. This was my church and it was everything I liked about ministry, but I didn't feel rejected at all – how could I with a 100% vote from the people that mattered? That 71% was more than I expected, so as much as I didn't want to leave, I did get a good vote. And to be fair to the Methodist Church, when it came to stationing, of the 31 Methodist Districts 15 of them requested me! That's nearly half! They redeemed themselves with that!

But I was in Eastbourne, I upset a few Methodists – it was a fairly liberal circuit and I always upset liberals, but I've come to live with that. I also developed my ministry a lot and when the time was over I found it hard to move on, especially as I moved to a traditional circuit that was just going through the motions, with older congregations and a traditional approach to church. In the Haven I was always doing something different. There were many times that I was told that I was '*just right*' for planting this church. This was where I belonged. I was at home! There were occasions when I went to Methodist District events and there would be small groups talking about Fresh Expressions of Church and after a while we would introduce ourselves and when I said I was from the Haven there would always be someone there who would say, 'Oh, is that you?'. My church had a certain fame – we were doing what we were supposed to be doing.

Of course that didn't last, but it is the time I look back on as the defining time of my ministry. I was there for 9 years. When I had to look at leaving I applied for the Methodist Church's new scheme of Pioneer Ministers – Venture FX. This was to recruit people to plant churches like the Haven with people in the age-group that the Haven had – and I was turned down. And I thought – well, that's the Methodist Church!

The only story from my Eastbourne time I want to concentrate on came about with the help of one of the Hailsham Methodists before I moved down to

Eastbourne. This particular man was a retired solicitor and when I visited him in his country mansion he showed me his family-tree research. I had a standing joke at the time that went:

'I'm researching my family tree'
'Oh, really, how far have you got?'
'Well, I've found my mother!'

And so I told Phil about this and he offered to write to her, on his headed paper. And so he did. He asked if she was … formerly … born in … If so would she get in touch? She thought she had inherited some money so she rang him instantly. (I'm not making that up; she admitted it later).

He told her the real reason for writing and her husband said there was no chance that I could contact her – it was all in the past. My immediate reaction was: *'It might be in the past for you, but it is my life'*. I think curiosity overcame her, so she agreed to contact me. She sent me a card for my 40th birthday, with some photographs of herself around the time I was born. That was a strange experience. It was clouded by the fact that it wasn't a birthday card – it was a scene of the Lake District. And she signed it with her first name. I had no expectations, but when you haven't seen your mother for 40 years you don't expect to be on first name terms with her. And again as Nancy Verrier writes: *'being rejected for the second time is devastating for the adoptee'*. It didn't devastate me, but it did concern me that I felt nothing.

This woman was the cause of all my problems and I felt nothing, at first.

And then I 'phoned her. I can remember dialling the number and hesitating over the last number for a long time before I pressed it. It was a strained conversation, but we agreed to meet; in the Lake District. We parked in the same car park. Her husband came with her because he didn't trust me. When I first met her she was complaining that she had to pay to park. I should have realised then. She told me my hair was too long, and I really should have caught on then. She was 40 years too late to tell me anything, but she didn't seem to realise that. I spent a long time analysing my feelings at meeting this woman and it was really difficult because I felt nothing. I didn't feel happy, or relieved; I didn't feel angry. I know, as time went on, that I was disappointed. She was not what I was expecting (I was expecting someone like me) and she was not what I was hoping for. Now, to be clear: I had no hopes, but I started this search when Jenny from Yorkshire died. I don't get emotional at funerals, but I had tears in my eyes taking Jenny's funeral and I realised that she is what I was hoping for. Remember Peter Pan's Lost Boys singing that song about, *'Who needs a mother'*? They finish by singing, *'I do'*. Well, that is how I felt, but this wasn't the mother I needed. I tried. I really tried. We went to her house, we met her daughter, who was about 2 years younger than me and her son who was 3 years younger and I tried to imagine what it would have been like growing up with them. And that was difficult, because I realised that all my experiences and my reactions to them, have made me who I am. If she hadn't given me away I wouldn't have the rejection problem, but would her husband have wanted her with a baby? Impossible to say.

There was one time when she was visiting us in Hailsham and I had shown her some baby photographs and early school photographs of me. I left the room and when I came back in she was looking at the photographs with tears in her eyes. She said that giving me up was the hardest thing she had done. But that was it; there was no feeling.

Anyway, it lasted for two years. I was told that two years is normal or average. Ours ended when she 'phoned one night and told me it had been my turn to 'phone. I said that I hadn't realised there were rules. She informed me that there were and it was up to me to 'phone next time. I haven't heard from her since and so I'm guessing she doesn't know where I live anymore, although my mobile number hasn't changed. I have been rejected a second time and it hasn't affected me at all. I think all along I expected her to act this way. Having analysed it occasionally for the past 10 years I think the biggest disappointment was that she didn't say sorry. But I wish I had never contacted her. I grew up without any curiosity and with no desire to ever find her. My adopted dad always wanted me to want this and he even offered to find her for me, but that was more to do with his issues than with mine. I think I would have felt better never knowing. She never asked me what life had been like for me. Maybe she was afraid I would tell her it was good, but as I said, I can't write about other people's motives and thoughts – only mine. I would have liked her to ask what it was like growing up after she had abandoned me. Maybe that's asking too much! But she put me in that position. There really was no bond between us; I couldn't detect any feelings in her at all.

But that is it really. I'll mention one last healing account and then conclude the story. When I moved to Eastbourne one of the 'church planting team' had a sore shoulder and I offered to pray and lay hands on her. These people wanted to be charismatics, but they had never experienced anything like this and so embarrassment and childish giggling followed, but no healing. It was another couple of years before I saw anyone healed, but once that started we had a few significant ones.

But before I left Yorkshire the group that organised the healing nights decided they should pray for me to be healed. I couldn't tell if anything happened, but 2 years into being in Hailsham I read of a new blood test that could detect coeliac antibodies in the blood stream, so I went to my GP and told him I wanted to do an experiment to check out this healing. Fortunately he was open-minded and so I ate everything I had been missing for the last 4 years. Two weeks later I had a blood test and there was no sign of the antibodies. Just to be sure I said I wanted to try another 2 weeks and so the 2nd blood test came back negative. I was healed. I put on another half stone then. Twice when I had coeliac disease I ate the wrong thing and the pain had been agonising. Now there was no more pain. By the way, my leg pain turned out to be sciatica and that has never gone away.

Then in my final year in Eastbourne I had gone to the cinema in Brighton Marina with Anne and Tamar and as I was driving home I had bad chest pains – heart attack-style pains. I managed to carry on driving and by the morning they had gone. This was now Saturday morning. By Saturday evening the pains were back, but Sunday morning they were gone, so I got through the church service OK. Sunday evening they were back, Monday morning gone, Monday evening back. Tuesday was the start of the Christian Resource Exhibition in Esher in Surrey – a two hour drive away. We normally went two or three times in the week this exhibition was on, but I found myself drained of energy on this Tuesday. I had to keep sitting down and taking rests.

When it came time to leave at 5pm we had barely driven out of town when the pains started up again. By the time we got to the M23 heading into Brighton I could barely talk and I was having trouble breathing. Anne suggested driving to Brighton hospital, but I was convinced I could make it home. I didn't! We drove to

Eastbourne District General Hospital and I was taken to A&E to be poked and prodded until I was finally taken to a ward at 2am. They told me I had a Pulmonary Embolism. This was when I started hearing stories of people who had died of one of these blood clots.

So I was lying on the bed for several days wondering if I would survive and also reviewing my life. If this was it, was I ready? Well, yes I was. When I got back to my church the next Sunday, one of the church members said, '*You must have been scared*'. I asked, '*Why?*' and she realised what she had said. I'm a Christian; what is there to fear?

It made me wonder what I had achieved and whether or not I had fulfilled the purpose that God had for sparing me. My mother failed, in our reconciliation, because she never once said she was sorry for giving me away – that was all I wanted to hear. She blamed society, but she took no responsibility. She gave me the impression that if the 1967 Abortion Act had been passed in 1961 I wouldn't be here. But I am, and so I had to ask, as Captain James T Kirk did, as he was dying: '*Did (I) make a difference?*'

I asked my church that in my final service at the Haven: did I make a difference? They said I had made a difference to them and when I finished they gave me a standing ovation – it never was a normal church!

But 7 months later, snowed in in the North of Scotland I decided to write it all down, just to show what God can do.

I'm here today because God rescued me so many times, and no matter what people say to me, or about me, He still accepts me. One of those books I read by John Powell when I was first converted is called, *'Why Am I Afraid To Tell You Who I Am?'* He gives the answer in the book: 'because you may not like me and this is all I have'.

I am no longer afraid to tell you who I am; you may not like me; but God does and that is enough for me.